Social Work in a
Digital Society

Social Work in a Digital Society

SUE WATLING
JIM ROGERS

Series Editors: Jonathan Parker and Greta Bradley

 SAGE | **LearningMatters**

Los Angeles | London | New Delhi
Singapore | Washington DC

Learning Matters
An imprint of SAGE Publications Ltd
1 Oliver's Yard
55 City Road
London EC1Y 1SP

SAGE Publications Inc.
2455 Teller Road
Thousand Oaks, California 91320

SAGE Publications India Pvt Ltd
B 1/I 1 Mohan Cooperative Industrial Area
Mathura Road
New Delhi 110 044

SAGE Publications Asia-Pacific Pte Ltd
3 Church Steet
#10–04 Samsung Hub
Singapore 049483

Editor: Luke Block
Development Editor: Kate Lodge
Production Controller: Chris Marke
Project Management: Deer Park Productions,
Tavistock, Devon
Marketing Manager: Tamara Navaratnam
Cover Design: Code 5
Typeset by: Pantek Media, Maidstone, Kent
Printed by: TJ International Ltd, Padstow, Cornwall

Professional Capabilities Framework diagram
reproduced with permission of The College of
Social Work

Library of Congress Control Number:
2012933566

British Library Cataloguing in Publication Data

A catalogue record for this book is available from
the British Library

ISBN: 978 0 85725 844 1
ISBN: 978 0 85725 677 5 (pbk)

Contents

About the authors

Sue Watling is a Learning and Teaching Co-ordinator in the Centre for Educational Research and Development (CERD) at the University of Lincoln. As well as supporting staff in the design and delivery of inclusive and accessible online learning opportuniities, Sue teaches and researches on the social impact of the internet and digital inclusion. Her qualifications include a BA in Social Science, an MA in Gender Studies and an MA in Open and Distance Education. Currently undertaking PhD research into digital inclusion, Sue is a Fellow of the Higher Education Academy (HEA), a member of the Association for Learning Development in Higher Education (ALDinHE) and holds Learning Technologist certification with the Association for Learning Technology (CMALT).

Jim Rogers is a Senior Lecturer in the School of Health and Social Care at the University of Lincoln. He teaches on a range of undergraduate and postgraduate social work and nursing programmes, particularly those with a mental health focus, and has professional qualifications in mental health nursing (RMN), complementary medicine (RS Hom), Higher Education teaching and learning, and an MSc in Health Sciences Research from the University of York. Jim is a Fellow of the Higher Education Academy (HEA) and his research interests include aspects of personalisation; mental capacity issues; complementary medicine and the use of homeopathy; addictions, particularly the prevalence and impact of gambling problems and inequalities like the growth of digital divides. Jim is currently researching the impact of the new Deprivation of Liberty Safeguards on care homes in Lincolnshire and the effect of digital developments on local social work practice.

Series editors' preface

The Western world, including the UK, faces numerous challenges over forthcoming years, many of which are brought to the fore by ever-developing technologies that become out-dated as quickly as they become part of everyday realities. Challenges also include dealing with the impact of an increasingly ageing population, with its attendant social care needs, and working with the financial implications that such a changing demography brings, and learning new social performances to effect care or to stay in contact with others. At the other end of the lifespan the need for high-quality childcare, welfare and safeguarding services have been highlighted as society develops and responds to a changing complex-ion. National and global perturbations have continued to be influenced by social media and technologies. The contemporary world demands engagement with such and social work needs also to respond.

Migration has increased as a global phenomenon and we now live and work with the implications of global issues in our everyday and local lives. Often these issues influence how we construct our social services and determine what services we need to offer, includ-ing the ways in which we offer these services. It is likely that as a social worker you will work with a diverse range of people throughout your career, many of whom have expe-rienced significant, and traumatic, events that require a professional and caring response grounded, of course, in the laws and social policies that have developed as a result. As well as working with individuals, however, you may be required to respond to the needs of a particular community disadvantaged by world events or excluded within local com-munities because of assumptions made about them, and you may be embroiled in some of the tensions that arise from implementing policy-based approaches that may conflict with professional values. What is clear within these contexts is that you may be working with a range of people who are often at the margins of society, socially excluded or in need of protection and safeguarding. Technologies may be useful in dealing with some of these issues but may also be implicated in the further marginalisation of those people with whom social workers practise. This book provides important knowledge and informa-tion to help you become aware of these issues, and to respond appropriately when faced with new technologies, older technologies and challenging situations.

The importance of social work education came to the fore again following the inquiry into the death of baby Peter and the subsequent report from the Social Work Task Force set up in its aftermath. It is timely, also, to reconsider elements of social work education as it is being taken forward by the Reform Board process in England and its implementation – indeed, we should view this as a continual striving for excellence! Reflection, revision and reform allow us to focus clearly on what knowledge is useful to engage with in learning to be a social worker, and using information technologies are part of this: social workers are part of digital society. The focus on 'statutory' social work, and by dint of that involuntary clients, brings to the fore the need for social workers to be well versed in the mechanisms and nuances of legislation that can be interpreted and applied to empower, protect and assist, but also to understand the social policy arena in which practice is forged. This important book provides readers with a beginning sense of the complexities and anomalies of digital society and its connections with contemporary social work.

The books in this series respond to the agendas driven by changes brought about by professional body, Government and disciplinary review. They aim to build on and offer introductory texts based on up-to-date knowledge and social policy development and to help communicate this in an accessible way, preparing the ground for future study as you develop your social work career. The books are written by practitioners and academics who are passionate about social work and social services and aim to instil that passion in others. The knowledge introduced in this book is important for all social workers in all fields of practice as they seek to reaffirm social work's commitment to those it serves.

Professor Jonathan Parker, Bournemouth University

Greta Bradley, University of York

Introduction

This book is written for a range of social work and social care students who are in education or placement and developing the necessary knowledge and understanding of the many different guises of social exclusion. It will also be of interest to all social workers and anyone else working in the field of social care. It is designed to introduce a potential new category of twenty-first-century disadvantage and exclusion; one brought about through the impact of a digital society, in particular the influence of the internet.

The first decade of the twenty-first century has witnessed a massive shift to digital ways of working. These have infiltrated individual lifestyles as well as almost every aspect of education and professional practice. We have all been influenced by the development of digital technologies and the move to online communication and provision of information. However, as is often the case in times of great change, the demands of day-to-day living mean we can be so busy adapting and coping with new ways of working, we are often unaware of the broader social significance of these changes. The book examines how social work practice is being challenged by such changes, in particular the ethical issues of unequal access to resources and how digital divides are exacerbating existing categories of social exclusion, creating the potential for further marginalisation and disempowerment as public services move to online design and delivery. It critically examines the impact of a digital society on its citizens, in particular the government's ongoing shift to digital-by-default policy, and the potential implications of digital exclusion for service users. The essential requirements of digital literacies for students, educators and practitioners runs throughout any conversation regarding social work in a digital society and they are included here in this book. Of particular importance is the need for confidence and competence with digital environments, accurate evaluation of online content, awareness of the difference between private and public online identities, and offering appropriate support for the service user who is increasingly being presented with digital technologies to support independent living.

While the book is primarily aimed at social work students in their first year or level of study, it will also be useful for students in subsequent years, depending on how programmes have been designed and the order in which they are approached. It will be particularly useful for students preparing for practice learning as this is where the need for caution with personal digital behaviours is essential and the reality of exclusion from digital information and public services may first be encountered. The book will appeal to people considering a career in social work or social care but not yet studying for a social work degree, as well as assisting students undertaking a range of social and health care courses in further education. Nurses, occupational therapists and other health and social care professionals will be able to gain an insight into the new requirements demanded of social workers with regard to the social impact of digital technologies and their parameters of access. Experienced and qualified social workers, especially those contributing to practice learning, will also be able to use this book for consultation, teaching, revision and to gain an insight into the expectations of digital confidence and competence raised by the qualifying degree in social work. Unless stated otherwise, the examples used throughout the book apply to the UK.

Requirements for social work education

Social work education has undergone a major transformation to ensure that qualified social workers are educated to honours degree level and develop knowledge, skills and values which are common and shared. A vision for social work operating in complex human situations has been adopted. This is reflected in the following definition from the International Association of Schools of Social Work and International Federation of Social Workers:

> *The social work profession promotes social change, problem solving in human relationships and the empowerment and liberation of people to enhance well-being. Utilising theories of human behaviour and social systems, social work intervenes at the points where people interact with their environments. Principles of human rights and social justice are fundamental to social work.*

(IFSW, 2001)

While there is a great deal packed into this definition it encapsulates the notion that social work concerns individual people and wider society. Social workers practise with people who are vulnerable, who are struggling in some way to participate fully in society and have equal access to necessary resources. Social workers walk that tightrope between the marginalised individual and the social and political environment which may have contributed to their marginalisation. With regard to digital divides, the social worker will frequently find themselves in the unique position of seeing both sides of the inclusion and exclusion paradox which is inherent in the development of new technologies. They will also find they occupy a space of privilege whereby they are generators of digital content so need to ensure exclusion is neither replicated nor reinforced by their own digital practices.

As a social worker, you will need to be highly skilled and knowledgeable to work effectively within a digital society. Previous and present governments have been keen for social work education and practice to improve and keep up to date with contemporary practices. In order to improve the quality of professional social work, it is crucial that student social workers develop a rigorous grounding in and understanding of relevant theories and models. Such knowledge helps social workers know what to do, when to do it and how to do it, while recognising that social work is a complex activity with no absolute 'rights' and 'wrongs' of practice for each situation. This book subscribes to a social barriers model, often specifically linked with a disabling environment, and views digital divides as having social and cultural foundations rather than technological ones. The need for developing an understanding of the social shaping of digital technologies is of particular relevance to the social work profession with its focus on individual empowerment. The book has been written against the background of work carried out by the Social Work Reform Board implementing the recommendations made by the Social Work Task Force to improve the quality of social work, which has included revising and renewing the quality and consistency of the social work degree with an aim to improve the expertise of social work graduates and ensure you are all best prepared for the demands of a changing society. Recognising how digital ways of working are becoming integral to social work education and professional practice, the book supports those recommendations which help *improve the learning experiences of students and result in graduates who are suitable and better prepared to undertake the demanding and complex challenges of social work today* (Department for Education, 2010, p4).

The book will help social work students meet the information, communication, technology and numeracy subject skills identified in the Quality Assurance Agency (QAA) academic benchmark criteria for social work (QAA, 2008). Benchmark 5.9 states, *The student is able to use ICT knowledge and skills effectively in a professional practice context* and specific criteria include demonstrating the ability to:

- use ICT effectively for professional communication, data storage and retrieval and information searching;
- use ICT in working with people who use services;
- demonstrate sufficient familiarity with statistical techniques to enable effective use of research in practice;
- integrate appropriate use of ICT to enhance skills in problem-solving;
- apply numerical skills to financial and budgetary responsibilities;
- have a critical understanding of the social impact of ICT, including an awareness of the impact of the 'digital divide'.

The book has an action-oriented approach which will help facilitate evaluation and review of your development as a digitally literate social work student both during your studies and while on practice placement. Research summaries will introduce you to key thinking behind both the development of the internet and the impact of a digital society on lifestyles, education and professional practice. Case studies, which focus predominantly on the experience of service users, will be used throughout to enhance these processes and to illustrate key points.

Structure of the book

This book is designed to help you gain knowledge about the impact of a digital society on individual lifestyles and ways of working. In particular it is concerned with the differential access parameters which create digital exclusion and the potential implications of these for social work education and practice. The book is concerned with you achieving the confidence and competence to operate effectively within digital environments, to recognise the benefits technology has to offer while also being aware of the potential disadvantages in terms of barriers to access. As society moves towards increasingly digital ways of working, so the social work profession will inevitably become involved with issues of digital inclusion, in particular where service users are being denied equitable access to online sources of information and the digital management of welfare services.

The book contains six chapters covering the social impact of the internet, contemporary digital policy and practice, digital equalities and digital divides, social work education, social work placement and practice and digital literacies.

In the first chapter, the social impact of the internet, you will be introduced to some of the ways in which digital technologies have influenced access to information and communication, and how the open nature of the internet poses challenges to traditional conceptions of public and private domains. As social workers you will find it useful to be aware of the risks as well as the benefits of being online and how best to stay safe both for yourselves and for service users. We will examine the permanence of digital footprints, introduce the concept of the 'social shaping' of technology and include some of the psychosocial consequences which result when virtual worlds mirror and amplify behaviours found in real ones. The chapter shows how social work students and practitioners may find themselves in a unique position to experience both sides of the digital divide. You will be adopting increasingly digital ways of working and managing access to digital resources, while those experiencing marginalisation and social disadvantage are most likely to become digitally excluded as well.

Chapter 2 looks at contemporary digital policy and practice and introduces government directives for digital-by-default access to public services. Driven by incentives to cut costs and increase efficiency, services such as housing, health care and the payment of welfare benefits are increasingly moving towards digital delivery of resources. The chapter will look at government incentives set up to encourage people to shift to digital lifestyles and practices. It will focus on the reality of this shift for those without the prerequisite skills or means of access and show how existing laws and policies can help social workers to advocate and empower service users towards equitable digital inclusion.

In Chapter 3 we address digital equalities and digital divides through the lens of the social barriers model which was introduced by the disability rights movement in the 1990s. A barriers model views the external environment as disabling, in particular where access parameters do not take into account wide enough diversity or difference. This chapter introduces some of the assistive technology used to enable independence and examines some of the ethical issues this raises. It looks at how assistive technologies can support individual interaction with computers and the internet, examining in particular the paradox between technology which supports and enables digital access and the environmental barriers which prevent that access from taking place.

Chapter 4 examines social work education and tools for virtual learning in a digital age, in particular the relationship between digital technologies and the social work curriculum. You will have many opportunities to ensure you are equipped with the confidence and competence to operate effectively within a digital society. The chapter looks at the impact of virtual learning environments, of electronic portfolios and a range of Web 2.0 style tools for teaching, learning and research. All these can be used to enhance your learning and the adoption of the processes of critical reflective practice which are integral to both higher education and social work. The chapter also introduces the latest research which suggests digital ways of working are changing the ways in which the brain processes and analyses information, and shows how your own critical engagement with digital ways of working can help develop awareness of the social impact of digital exclusion, especially for the service users you may soon be working with on placement and in practice.

In Chapter 5 we move on to social work placements and practice and the digital ways of working you might encounter there. The chapter addresses the use of online social media such as Facebook and the need for strict boundaries between personal and professional communication. It looks at the impact of digital practices on a range of services and how social workers need to enable the advantages of technology while being aware of the parameters of digital exclusion where access is problematic or denied.

Chapter 6 addresses the topic of digital literacies which are core to the higher education experience and professional practice. It pays attention to the application of critical thinking and reflection towards digital ways of working. You will be encouraged to ask questions and question the answers in order to authenticate your experiences online and validate the digital content you might find there. A key feature of the internet is how we are no longer passive consumers of information, but have become active generators of digital content via blogs, wikis and other forms of social media. A result is that we need to distinguish between personal and professional online identities and ensure we do not inadvertently compound existing exclusion through the ways in which we operate online. Threshold concepts are introduced in this chapter. They are used to demonstrate awareness of how the differential nature of digital exclusion can be increased and ensure the appropriate graduate attributes for working and living in a digital age.

Throughout the chapters there are links to appropriate websites containing additional information alongside recommendations for further reading. All chapters conclude with bulleted summary points. The final chapter revisits the main themes of the book, with further signposts for using the internet to support your continual development as a social work practitioner in a digital age.

You are encouraged to work through the book as an active participant, taking responsibility for your learning, in order to increase your knowledge, understanding and ability to apply this learning to practice. You will be expected to reflect creatively on your own digital literacies and the importance of inclusive digital practice. Case studies throughout the book introduce you to a variety of different digital technologies including their advantages and disadvantages. We have devised activities that require you to reflect on your own experiences with digital ways of working. This knowledge will help develop your awareness of the impact of a digital society and enhance your understanding of the construction of digital divides. Finally, the book will encourage you to maintain a critical approach to both present and potential digital developments and the role we can all play in ensuring our digital practices neither replicate nor reinforce existing exclusion.

It is worth bearing in mind as you read this book that digital environments change very quickly. The internet and the world wide web are fast-moving places where new developments in software, and in the design and delivery of digital resources, mean there is never a point where anything can be seen as finished or complete. We have tried to make the content as up to date as possible but there will inevitably be instances where information given may have been superseded. The speed at which digital ways of working are taking over from traditional practices provided the impetus for this book. This is also one of the reasons why the book has particular relevance for social work students, educators and professional practitioners who work with service users on a regular basis. It is the service users themselves who have to manage with increasingly digital policies and practices and deal with unequal parameters of access to online resources. We have done our best to continually revise the text right up to the last moment before printing but it is an almost impossible task. If on reading this it seems that there are examples of outdated information then we do apologise.

This book has been carefully mapped to the new Professional Capabilities Framework for Social Workers in England and will help you to develop the appropriate standards at the right level. These standards are:

- **Professionalism** – Identify and behave as a professional social worker committed to professional development.

- **Values and ethics** – Apply social work ethical principles and values to guide professional practice.

- **Diversity** – Recognise diversity and apply anti-discriminatory and anti-oppressive principles in practice.

- **Justice** – Advance human rights and promote social justice and economic wellbeing.

- **Knowledge** – Apply knowledge of social sciences, law and social work practice theory.

- **Judgement** – Use judgement and authority to intervene with individuals, families and communities to promote independence, provide support and prevent harm, neglect and abuse.

- **Critical reflection and analysis** – Apply critical reflection and analysis to inform and provide a rationale for professional decision-making.

- **Contexts and organisations** – Engage with, inform, and adapt to changing contexts that shape practice. Operate effectively within your own organisational frameworks and contribute to the development of services and organisations. Operate effectively within multi-agency and inter-professional settings.

- **Professional leadership** – Take responsibility for the professional learning and development of others through supervision, mentoring, assessing, research, teaching, leadership and management.

References to these standards will be made throughout the text and you will find a diagram of the Professional Capabilities Framework in Appendix 1 at the end of the book.

Chapter 1

The social impact of the internet

We live in a digital society which has significantly changed the information landscape affecting every aspect of our lives. The current wave of technological innovation is part of the context in which social work students, practitioners and service users and carers operate.

(Rafferty and Steyaert, 2007, p165)

A C H I E V I N G   A   S O C I A L   W O R K   D E G R E E

This chapter will help you to develop the following capabilities, to the appropriate level, from the Social Work Professional Capabilities Framework.

- **Professionalism.** Identify and behave as a professional social worker committed to professional development.
- **Values and ethics.** Apply social work ethical principles and values to guide professional practice.
- **Diversity.** Recognise diversity and apply anti-discriminatory and anti-oppressive principles in practice.
- **Justice.** Advance human rights and promote social justice and economic well-being.
- **Knowledge.** Apply knowledge of social sciences, law and social work practice theory.
- **Judgement.** Use judgement and authority to intervene with individuals, families and communities to promote independence, provide support and prevent harm, neglect and abuse.
- **Critical reflection and analysis.** Apply critical reflection and analysis to inform and provide a rationale for professional decision-making.
- **Contexts and organisations.** Engage with, inform, and adapt to changing contexts that shape practice.
- **Professional leadership.** Take responsibility for the professional learning and development of others through supervision, mentoring, assessing, research, teaching, leadership and management.

See Appendix 1 for the Professional Capabilities Framework diagram.

The chapter will also introduce you to the following academic standards as set out in the 2008 Social Work Subject Benchmarks:
5.9 ICT and numerical skills.

Introduction

Few aspects of our daily lives do not involve the internet either directly or indirectly. The move to using digital forms of communication or information has all happened very quickly and it is easy to assume everyone is connected. However, this is not true and growing digital divides exist between those with access and those for whom that access is problematic or denied. Research suggests those who are socially excluded are also those most likely to experience barriers to digital resources and, in an increasingly digital society, this exclusion has the potential to compound existing inequalities. The current government is moving to digital-by-default management of public services. Already the majority of employment opportunities in the UK involve digital competencies in one form or another and there are few areas of home, work or education which have not been influenced by the affordances of the internet. Social work is no exception. Here digital practices have infiltrated what was traditionally a person-centred, face-to-face culture and we have all had to adapt to these new ways of working.

As social work students and practitioners you will need to develop a critical awareness of the impact of a digital society and the effect this has on marginalised sections of the population who have yet to engage with digital practices. You may find yourself in a unique position to see both sides of the digital divide and recognise how it involves complex issues with no 'one-size-fits-all' solution. In Chapter 3 we address the realities of digital exclusion in more detail. In this first chapter, we will introduce the broader social impact of digital ways of working. We will be looking at how digital technologies have influenced communication between families, friends and strangers and how the open nature of the internet, and its lack of rules or boundaries, can pose challenges to traditional conceptions of public and private domains. As we move closer towards the online management of our lives, the permanence of digital footprints will be highlighted and attention drawn to some of the psychosocial consequences which occur when virtual worlds mirror the attitudes and behaviours of people in real worlds. As social work students and practitioners you will find it useful to be aware of how being online offers risks as well as benefits and the steps we should all take to ensure safety during our travels into digital places.

RESEARCH SUMMARY

The difference between the internet and the world wide web

The internet consists of multiple digital connections between computer networks across the world. It began as a military communication system in the 1960s under the name ARPANET before evolving into civilian use by university networks in the 1980s and domestic owners of personal computers in the 1990s. The internet has remained independent of state or personal controls and is open to everyone with the means of access.

The world wide web describes the digital content distributed on the internet via websites. The code which lies behind web pages and the system of hyperlinks between them was invented by Tim Berners Lee in the late 1980s. The world wide web was originally envisioned as a free digital democratic space where everyone could participate in communication and the sharing of information. However, this early altruism has been challenged

Continued

RESEARCH SUMMARY continued

by capitalist economies to an extent where the commercial aspect of the internet has now become its primary characteristic and even its users have themselves become commodities. Search Engine Optimisation (SEO) ranks sites in order of their popularity in order to charge premium rates to advertisers. Information about the places users visit online and the choices they make there is recorded and used to make predictions to encourage future commercial transactions. It is important to be aware of how large companies monitor our online movements in order to try to influence our behaviour. However, alongside debates on the advantages and disadvantages of the internet and the world wide web, we need to remember that opportunities for participation are not universal. The more we move towards digital lifestyles and practices, the more significant are the divides between those with digital access and those for whom that access is problematic or denied.

The social impact of the internet

Internet-enabled lifestyles constitute radical social change but we can be so busy juggling the multiple commitments of home, care, work and study, that the full implications of these changes may pass us by. Take a few minutes to consider the extent to which you communicate and access information online, in particular in terms of shopping, banking, booking travel tickets and keeping in touch with other people. You will soon realise just how much a digital screen has replaced traditional face-to-face transactions. New generations are growing up at ease with online environments and view mobile connection to the internet as integral to daily life. To see just how quickly these changes have taken place it can be useful to look back and mark those occasions when the names we now take for granted first entered our vocabulary. Yahoo was set up in 1994, followed by Amazon and Echo Bay (later known as eBay) in 1995, Hotmail in 1996 and Google and PayPal in 1998. Following these early pioneers, the first decade of the twenty-first century witnessed an exponential rise in digital ways of working, with many of the brand names we now instantly recognise being developed in a comparatively short period of time.

Below is a list of the key players who have been instrumental in changing the ways in which we access digital information and communication and have moved towards digital ways of working.

2000 TripAdvisor made use of interactive travel forums to share information on travel and hotels.

2000 Blogger offered free blogging software with the potential for making digital authors out of everyone with access.

2001 Wikipedia launched an ambitious attempt to create an encyclopaedia of knowledge based on harvesting the collective expertise of individual users.

2001 StumbleUpon was a new style of search engine which filtered results in order to make recommendations based on individual subject preferences.

2002 LinkedIn became one of the first business-oriented social networking sites.

9

2002 TinyURL was the first URL shortening service which made it easier to manage lengthy website addresses.

2002 Skyscanner offered a comparison service for flights which included both price and airport location.

2003 Skype launched free telephone calls over the internet using an intuitive, user-friendly interface which later incorporated video via webcams.

2003 MySpace was one of the first social networking sites for young people which specialised in music and supporting creative and artistic ventures.

2003 iTunes established its online store selling downloadable access to music and videos.

2003 Second Life launched an avatar-driven 3D multimedia virtual world.

2004 Digg was developed to collect and distribute individual lists of bookmarked sites, creating the trend for social bookmarking taken up by similar software such as Reddit and Delicious.

2004 The Facebook, later known as Facebook, was set up in the US initially for college students but soon spread to become an international social networking phenomenon.

2004 Flickr was set up in 2004 as a social networking site, based on sharing photographs and videos which can be categorised through tagging, making it easier to group like with like and for users to search using their own preferences.

2005 YouTube video streaming and the rise in mobile video capture devices came together in this program which supported the uploading and sharing of short video clips.

2005 Google Earth launched in a format accessible by home computers and made available images of countries sourced from satellite and aerial imagery. This was closely followed by Google Maps which offered street maps and a route planning service.

2006 Twitter was set up in 2006 as a social networking service supporting micro-blogging via posts known as Tweets; each Tweet is limited to a maximum of 140 characters.

2006 WikiLeaks took advantage of the collaborative editing facilities of the wiki and began to publish media which was classified as secret but submitted anonymously.

2007 Google Street View used the technology already featured in Google Maps and Google Earth to provide street-level views in towns and cities across the world.

2007 The Kindle e-book reader was launched by Amazon alongside the Amazon e-book service.

2009 Google set up Google Docs, a free data storage service which allows users to share and collaborate online.

2010 Apple iPad was launched offering a range of internet services in a mobile format.

These changes have all happened very quickly and the full implications of a digital society are not yet known; however, there are growing concerns that not all of these digital developments might be beneficial.

In the early days of the internet, the design of digital data was restricted to computer specialists who understood the specific Hyper Text Markup Language (HTML) code required to build websites. Early web pages consisted primarily of text and the environment was a 'read-only' one; apart from chat rooms and email there was little opportunity for interaction or individual contribution. Today, the internet has evolved into what is known as a Web 2.0 environment hosting a variety of interactive software like blogs and wikis, all of which support user-generated content and file sharing. This means that anyone with access to the internet can contribute to the world wide web, resulting in an almost unimaginable volume of content. It has become increasingly difficult to separate formal knowledge and information from personal opinion and fantasy but this is now an essential skill, in particular for those working in higher education and in professional practice. You will find more information about using the internet effectively in Chapters 4 and 6. Here in this chapter we are going to examine some of the more generic social aspects of being online and operating safely within digital environments.

The internet can connect people from all across the world whether they are families, friends, colleagues or strangers. While this offers a digital means of keeping in touch through email or webcams, it has also increased the potential for unwanted communication such as cyberbullying, a new and potentially serious attack on individual privacy and well-being, and we will be returning to this later in the chapter. Another consequence of using the internet is the permanence of our digital footprints. There are few controls over public access to personal digital data. This means we don't know who is looking at information about us and we cannot be sure what that information is or even where it has come from. Cybercrime is the name given to online criminal activity directed at misuse of personal data and we will be examining some examples of this. Finally, the internet is blurring distinctions between public and private domains and we all need to be aware of the boundaries between personal and professional online practices. It is important to remember that for all the affordances of the internet, its content and use constitutes a mirror of society in all its strengths and weaknesses. As social work students and practitioners we need to be knowledgeable about the positive and negative impacts of a digital society, in particular how to ensure the online safety of those participating in new digital ways of working. We also need to demonstrate a critical awareness of the parameters of access in order to highlight and challenge digital discrimination in the same way we would challenge any other form of marginalisation and disempowerment which led to unequal access to resources.

RESEARCH SUMMARY

The 'social shaping' of technology

It is important to be critical about the role of technology in society and understand how the internet and the world wide web are social products shaped by the political, economic and cultural environment in which they are produced and embedded. Adoption of new technologies is never instant; instead, it always happens in stages. Rogers (2006) has produced a 'diffusion of innovations' model which shows how change is led by the Innovators (2.5 per cent) and Early Adopters (13.5 per cent), followed by the Early

Continued

RESEARCH SUMMARY *continued*

Majority (34 per cent) and then the Late Majority (34 per cent), and finally the Laggards (16 per cent). This model is useful for showing the adoption of change as a process but it must be remembered that the process may be influenced by pre-existing social arrangements and many late adopters are denied participation through no fault of their own. As society moves towards increased reliance on the internet for the delivery and management of welfare services, we need to pay attention to the differential access parameters known as digital divides or structural information inequalities (van Dijk, 2005). Social power is increasingly centred on individual positioning within digital media networks while the internet privileges those with easy access to information and communication technologies. The move towards welfare services which are digital by default has potential implications for the social work profession because digital technologies are not neutral. They favour those who can afford to participate and have the means to operate within a narrow range of access criteria. Government initiatives which fail to address the underlying causes of digital exclusion can only result in marginalised sections of society experiencing further disadvantage and continuing to be disempowered.

The internet and communication

The internet supports anonymity when communicating with others. It is possible to hide behind an email address like 123456789@gmail.com and communicate in ways you might not in a face-to-face situation. A false identity also enables users to be critical and engage in unprofessional behaviours. For example, the internet hosts numerous blogs written by people employed within the public sector who have taken advantage of a false identity to talk about their work with candour and there are situations where this might be useful. While the internet supports all types of communication without censorship, we need to bear in mind the key differences between honest reflection, constructive criticism and abuse. Anonymity can make people careless about what they say in online environments and email has become notorious for expressions of emotion, often anger or frustration, being sent in haste without pausing to reflect on the potential consequences of what has been written. Classic workplace email errors include sending a 'Reply to All' rather than replying to an individual, or being indiscreet about a work colleague or senior manager and finding someone else has forwarded the email on to a wider audience. The massive webs of electronic contacts addresses between people both in and out of the workplace means that not only do messages travel fast but also there is no way of stopping them. Once an email has left you, you have no control over where it goes or who reads it. Work emails need to be written in a neutral tone and never in haste. It is always wise to pause and re-read an email before sending or if it concerns a difficult subject, consider asking a colleague to read it through first.

Behaving badly online

Trolling is a term commonly used to describe online comments which are potentially harmful; in particular, the term is used to refer to the habit of posting negative comments on tribute websites set up in memory of young people who have died. In the UK, the Communications Act of 2003 governs the internet, email, mobile phone calls and text messaging and under Section 127 of the act it is an offence to send messages that are grossly offensive or of an indecent, obscene or menacing character. The offence occurs whether those targeted actually receive the message or not. If you Google the terms Trolling and Facebook you will find information about two people who have received jail sentences for posting inappropriate comments and obscene messages.

The word Troll derives from Norwegian folklore and refers to a monster; in the case of Trolling the reference is to the 'monstrous' behaviour. The reasons for behaving badly online are complex but when questioned people have quoted reasons including amusement, boredom and revenge. The activity may be part of the psychology of addiction whereby people feel rewarded for their actions. In the case of Trolling, being online helps people to feel anonymous and can break down inhibitions, thereby encouraging engagement with behaviours which might not otherwise have been considered but are rewarding to the perpetrator (Griffiths, 2010).

Trolling might also be exacerbated by the ways in which the internet and in particular social media are used to expose individual lifestyles and promote self-publicity. This openness can be interpreted by some people as provocative and risks exposing the individual to personal abuse. The internet is designed to support freedom of speech and with that power comes responsibility, but ultimately this is not something over which it is always possible to exercise control.

Social media

Social media is the name given to software such as blogs and wikis and social networking programs like Facebook and Twitter. They support what is called user-generated content through the use of a text-box-editor which converts text into the necessary code and enables online communication and the sharing of digital information such as photos, music files and videos. The majority of social media programs are free to download and many include a home page facility which can be customised by uploading pictures or selecting a design template. Readers interact through posting comments on other people's content and many social networks enable users to 'follow' or become 'friends' with other users, creating the potential for building up large digital networks of family, friends, colleagues and even strangers.

Different social media programs have unique characteristics and can cater for specific interests. Facebook began as a social forum for college friends in America and while it remains a focus for social communication, it is increasingly used by small businesses, in particular third-sector, not-for-profit organisations that benefit from a free source of advertising and potential fundraising. Twitter limits text comments to 140 characters or fewer. These short statements are known as Tweets and taking part is called Tweeting. Twitter is popular for reporting on current news events as they are happening, such as civil disturbance, natural disasters and wars. Other examples of social media include YouTube for videos, Flickr and Picasa for digital images, MySpace for music and the creative arts and LinkedIn for professional networking.

Social media has helped to open up the potential of the internet for enabling mass public sharing of private information. The internet has made us all into potential distributers of digital content but with that power comes responsibility. We could all become internet spies. It is not difficult to find an address and postcode online and use Google Earth to see where someone lives. From there it is only a small step to making assumptions about social status based on location and house appearance. Further information can be gained from putting the person's name into Google or searching for their profile on a social networking site like Facebook. When we use the internet we leave behind permanent digital footprints and these can be used to build a psychometric e-profile. When meeting someone for the first time, or interviewing someone for a job, it is no longer uncommon for their name to have been previously entered into Google to see what information is returned. It is worth remembering that nothing on the internet is private and there are advisory steps which should be taken to minimise the consequences of these blurred boundaries between public and private domains.

If you use social media, it is important to be aware of the privacy controls as they offer some restriction on the movement of your information. However, even setting these controls to the highest level might not be a sufficient safeguard as you cannot control the privacy settings of those who have access to your information. Social media support and encourage the 'status update', which reflects what you are doing or how you are feeling at any particular time. When other 'friends' are being candid and open about their personal thoughts and emotions, it can be easy to follow suit and make indiscreet throwaway comments on the spur of the moment without thinking about the consequences. For many people their online conversations are as real as those they have face to face, but what is said between friends online can also be shared and passed around the internet by others. Where this sharing is inappropriate, your messages may reach people who have different views about your opinions. Anything which could be considered derogatory or slanderous can take on a life of its own with serious professional consequences. It is worth bearing in mind that you should never post comments regarding work situations or make personal remarks about colleagues, customers or service users. People have been suspended and lost their jobs over digital indiscretions such as these. Be careful who you accept as digital 'friends' and be sure not to post personal identification details online, in particular the contact details of either yourself or other people. Avoid giving away dates of birth as these are the building blocks of personal identity and can be used inappropriately. When you are employed in a professional capacity as a social worker on practice placement or as a fully qualified social worker, you should not use social media in any way which might break confidentiality or lead to accusations of unprofessional conduct. There is more advice about the appropriate use of social media in placement and practice in Chapter 5.

As social work students and practitioners you will be encouraged to be critically reflective, to take time to pause and think about your learning, practice and placement experiences. These processes of reflection can feel contrary to the fast-paced world of internet communication where everything happens instantly. Considering the issues raised within this book will encourage you to reflect on your own online practices and be critical about the way in which online environments are used. Social workers have a professional responsibility to exercise discretion and this applies to online environments as well as offline situations. While you may believe your privacy settings are enough to protect you online, it needs to be remembered that digital data has a habit of turning up where you least expect it. While you might feel you have done enough to protect your own anonymity, it is almost impossible to control the ways in which other people may be sharing content you have created within their own online networks which you are not part of.

Cyberbullying

Bullying is not new but the internet has enabled new forms of personal abuse and intimidation known as cyberbullying. This can happen through any form of digital communication such as instant messaging, text messaging, email or a social media network; it commonly involves text or images intended to be hurtful or embarrassing and is frequently targeted at younger people. Online bullying is particularly cruel because of the permanence of digital data and the speed at which content can be shared. Cyberbullying may be invisible to all but the bullies and their victim. It is often anonymous or the bully will pass themselves off as being someone different from who they really are. There are many different forms of digital bullying which include harassing or 'flaming' someone in a chat room or posting embarrassing or humiliating videos online. Happy slapping describes how people use their mobile phones to film and share videos of physical attacks. Another internet-enabled form of cyberbullying is setting up profiles on social networking sites with the intention of deliberately making fun of someone or encouraging hostility.

All words can be hurtful but digital words can hurt even more particularly where the abusive comments are made by someone who hides behind anonymity. Cyberbullying cannot be prevented so it is important to know how best to deal with it and telling other people is always the first step. Internet Service Providers (ISPs) and mobile phone companies can put in place procedures to block abusive messages and texts, and physical or sexual threats should always be reported to the police. Individual software often has the facility to block instant messages and mail filters can be set up to block emails. Make sure you know how to do this so you can protect not only yourself but friends, colleagues and service users. Abusive messages should always be ignored as responding often exacerbates the situation and although it can be upsetting, it is worth advising people to keep evidence of cyberbullying in case it is needed in the future.

RESEARCH SUMMARY

Cyberbullying and suicide

Links between traditional cases of bullying and suicidal thoughts in the victim are well established. New research by Professor Sameer Hinduja and Professor Justin Patchin is now linking cases of cyberbullying on the internet with increased rates of suicide noted in the 10–19 age group among those who were regular internet users compared with those who were not. Social networking sites such as Facebook, MySpace and Bebo are thought to be playing a substantive role by providing opportunities for online abuse, and these threatening behaviours have been related to increases in reports of suicidal thoughts and actions. Peer harassment is a key component of cyberbullying and because the internet supports anonymity, this can make it easier for people to lose inhibitions, leading to increased cases of online bullying behaviours. The ways in which depression can lower individual sense of self-worth and increase personal feelings of hopeless- ness and loneliness may be precursors to suicidal thoughts and behaviours. Patchin and Hinduja's research suggests that young victims of traditional offline bullying were less likely to have attempted suicide compared with young victims of cyberbullying, who were more likely to have made suicide attempts. In recent years the media have covered a number of instances of teenage suicide which appear to be related to cyberbullying. Reports reveal unkind and cruel messages about the victim which had previously been posted and shared on social networking sites. Hinduja and Patchin conclude that while the instances of cyberbullying themselves cannot necessarily be interpreted as a direct sole cause of suicide, it is highly likely that they will exacerbate existing instability and depression in the minds of adolescents already struggling with stressful life circumstances (Hinduja and Patchin, 2010).

Where to go for help and support

You will find it useful to collect lists of places to go for online help and support if you are involved with issues concerning misuse of the internet. Below are a few sites which might be included on your list.

Child Exploitation and Online Protection CEOP Centre has an online reporting facility at www.ceop.police.uk/report-abuse

Online support for people experiencing cyberbullying is available at www.cybermentors. org.uk and www.old.digizen.org

Childline can be contacted online at www.childline.org.uk or by telephone on 0800 1111. Both methods provide opportunities to contact someone in private about cyber- bullying. The telephone number will not show up on the phone bill. Childline is managed by the NSPCC.

Chat danger

Key 'chat rooms' into Google and you will find a variety of opportunities for online syn- chronous, real-time communication. Human beings are social creatures and value conversation whether it be with family, friends or even strangers, and on the internet someone somewhere will always be available to talk online. Chat rooms are popular but staying safe is of paramount importance. There are frequent media stories about adults passing themselves off as someone different in a chat room and 'grooming' younger people with the intention of meeting and sexually abusing them. It is good advice to always remember that online 'friends' are still strangers. No matter how long you have been talking to someone or how friendly they seem to be, people online cannot be relied upon to be who they say they are. When people seem friendly and ask for personal information it can be tempting to reveal more than you normally would, but giving out contact details or other personal information online will make you vulnerable. Using an on-screen identity is sometimes recommended but when you think about this, the advice actually reinforces the danger of believing anyone is who they say they are in a chat room or other online situation.

Increasing government concerns about sex offenders approaching children over the internet and grooming and sexually assaulting them led to the Sexual Offences Act 2003 and bringing the sentence for grooming in line with other child sex offences with a maximum sentence of ten years. Further information about reporting online crime and staying safe online is available at the following websites.

The Crown Prosecution Service (CPS) website at www.cps.gov.uk includes a code of practice for all victims of crime.

The direct.gov site for public services includes information about using the internet. Go to www.direct.gov.uk and search for staying safe online.

The Childline website offers online support for victims of cyberbullying as well as other forms of child abuse at www.childline.org.uk

Created by the Child Exploitation and Online Protection Centre (CEOP), this site offers information for children, parents, carers and teachers about the good and the less good aspects of being online: www.thinkuknow.co.uk

CASE STUDY

Wife pretends to be 14-year-old girl online

In 2009, Cheryl Roberts, aged 61, pretended to be a 14-year-old girl online. In this guise, she was asked by her husband David Roberts, aged 68, to meet for sex. Mrs Roberts had become suspicious about the amount of time her husband was spending in his study and of a message which popped up on their computer while he was out. While Mr Roberts was chatting online, Mrs Roberts used a different computer in the living room and pretended to be a schoolgirl. Mr Roberts propositioned the 'girl', unaware he was chatting to his wife. Mrs Roberts was so shocked by the behaviour of her husband of almost 20 years she brought in the police, who seized his computer and found dozens of illegal child pornographic images. Mr Roberts admitted engaging in sexual activity in the presence of a child and making and possessing illegal images. He was given a three-year community order and banned from having access in person or online to under-18s. The couple have now separated and are getting divorced.

Source: www.bbc.co.uk/news

Offensive content

The open nature of the internet means it can easily be used for uploading offensive anti-social materials. These might be racist, violent or pornographic in nature or include abusive images. There are a number of different laws which seek to regulate online content such as this and three of them are listed below.

- Protection of Children Act 1978 ensures it is against the law to be in possession of indecent images of children.

- The Terrorism Acts 2000 and 2006 ensure it is an offence to incite hatred against any religious or ethnic group or share information that urges people to commit or help with acts of terrorism.

- Part 5 (Criminal Law) of the Criminal Justice and Immigration Act 2008 ensures it is illegal to be in possession of extreme pornographic images.

There are a number of websites where illegal internet content can be reported and three of these are listed below.

www.iwf.org.uk The internet Watch Foundation (IWF) has a UK hotline for reporting criminal online content. IWF works in partnership with the police, government, the online industry and the public to combat this type of material and have it removed. Reports to the IWF are confidential and can be submitted online anonymously.

www.reporting.direct.gov.uk This website is intended for the public to report any illegal terrorist or violent extremist information, pictures or videos they find online.

www.report-it.org.uk Hate crime motivated by hatred of a person's disability, race, religion, sexual orientation or transgender identity can be reported on this website.

Tracking internet activity

The open and free nature of the internet makes it easy for content of an offensive nature to be uploaded and shared and software has been developed to block potentially offensive content. It is increasingly common for browsers and search engines to contain filtering options or alternatively you may be familiar with the concept of software such as Net Nanny which is designed for parental controls over the internet activity of family members. Parental control software can block access to certain internet sites which are considered to be inappropriate, provide reports on activity, including transcripts of instant messaging and chat conversations, as well as set controls over access times and hours. When the software has been set up, email notifications can be sent to the family's site administrator which contains reports on all content deemed questionable. Monitoring facilities include bullying or hurtful language, profanity, attempts at direct contact questions and noting if personal information has been disclosed. The degree to which families can put in place internet surveillance is continually adapting to keep up with the times. For example, activities on social media such as Facebook and Twitter can now be tracked. What might be thought of as private online communication between friends can actually be monitored to an extent that all profiles visited on Facebook are recorded and notifications sent when family members change their profile including an image of what the new profile looks like. Controls over internet access are advertised by the companies which sell them as being about good parenting rather than spying or eavesdropping but you might like to critically reflect on where you consider the line should be drawn between the two. It is only a small step from having these means to control family activity on the internet to applying similar surveillance to the digital activities of the wider society.

CASE STUDY

Permanent digital records

Kevin has been a fully qualified social worker for several years. He doesn't bring paperwork home because he knows how important it is to keep data secure and protected. He is careful to encrypt all his digital data files at work and is scrupulous about locking away anything which is confidential. At home Kevin has had a family computer for several years and decides to upgrade to a new one. Because the old PC is clunky and slow he decides to take it to the recycling plant where digital equipment is disposed of. The family have been using the computer for shopping online and managing their household accounts so Kevin takes care to copy all the important content onto an external disk drive and delete everything on the computer before disposal. Kevin doesn't realise that when the local council recycle digital equipment it can change hands many times and his computer was eventually bought by someone with the expertise to access all his personal information and details. Kevin had deleted the files but he hadn't erased them from the hard disk. This is a common mistake and one of the reasons why the second-hand computer trade is so lucrative. As well as Kevin's passwords and bank details, the fraudster took details about Kevin's identity. Using these he ordered credit cards in Kevin's name and began buying goods online, running up several thousand pounds worth of debt. Before disposing of any computer it is worth taking advice or using specialist software to permanently remove all traces of data. Kevin followed all the guidelines and rules about personal data at work but failed to apply the same caution to his own information and became another victim of cybercrime.

Surveillance society

Most people are unaware of the extent to which their internet use can be tracked but, just as domestic internet controls can be set up at home, so corporations and governments can record and monitor activity on networks, personal computers and mobile phones. This internet-enabled surveillance raises many ethical issues around potential violation of privacy.

The extent and implications of a surveillance society, in particular for those citizens dependent on the state for welfare services, are often not fully realised. Digitisation has automated the closed-circuit television (CCTV) systems in towns and cities, ostensibly to detect or prevent crime, vandalism and terrorism, but these surveillance techniques are not limited to the monitoring of physical movements. Digital technologies such as smart cards are used to record individual activities and behaviours, with this information being used as a basis for policy decisions on benefits and rights, often without a full public debate. Personal information which is gathered through surveillance-based techniques is then used for influencing policy decisions with regard to the direction and targeting of welfare resources and services.

> *While the surveillance society provides us with benefits and rights, it also has negative consequences, some of which are stark and potentially irreversible. Any public debate about surveillance needs to consider its effects on privacy, ethics and human rights; its impact on social inclusion and exclusion; changes to levels of choice, power and empowerment; whether those running such systems can ever be held to account and whether surveillance processes are transparent or not.*

(Murakami-Wood and Ball, 2006, p13)

It is easy to think of our personal internet activity as private but this is far from the truth; in fact it may be better to think of all internet activity as taking place in public. There are a number of different ways in which everything we do online is monitored and recorded. ISPs give all individuals an Internet Protocol (IP) address through which all of our internet movements are tracked. However the internet is accessed, whether through mobile phone, wireless network, landline or Bluetooth, or from the home, the workplace or educational institution, the surveillance process begins as soon as connection to the internet is established.

Common means of internet surveillance include the use of 'cookies'. These are small software programs which online companies install on computers when the user logs in or registers for a service. Cookies track visited websites and locations in order to deliver targeted advertising, but as well as storing 'customised' information they also create a history of usage which can be considered an invasion of privacy. Since 2011 the law has changed so that all websites which use cookies must inform the user by posting a message on their home page. This will contain information about the purpose of cookies and the user must tick a box to show they have accepted cookies from that particular site. By July 2012 all websites should contain this information.

For information on digital tracking on the internet visit www.legislation.gov.uk and search for Privacy and Electronic Communications Regulations.

For more information about the new cookie regulations visit www.aboutcookies.org

To see an example of the new cookie information agreement go to the UK Information Commissioner's Office at www.ico.gov.uk

RESEARCH SUMMARY

Social impact of the internet

The democratic nature of the internet supports a free-for-all environment where there are . . . no gatekeepers to filter truth from fiction, genuine content from advertising, legitimate information from error or downright deceit (Keen, 2007, p65). Web 2.0 style user-generated content tools have resulted in a digital world where everyone is simultaneously broadcasting themselves and no one is listening (Keen, 2007, p15). Commercial incentives are the dominant drivers behind search engines such as Google which return a combination of the most popular content along with the searcher's previous online activity. The results are the aggregated preferences of individuals rather than being based on any scientific, peer reviewed knowledge. As well as this mass of unregulated content, another key consequence of a digital society is digital division, both in terms of access and the purposes that access is used for. Steyaert and Gould (2009) have written specifically about the social work profession and the changing faces of these digital divides. They describe the challenge posed by the differences in content preferences across different socio-economic groups, in particular relating to the expanding entertainment nature of the internet. Referring to a famous polemic claiming the media industry was dumbing down US culture (Postman, 1985), they conclude that without attention to appropriate digital literacy skills, socially vulnerable citizens will be at risk of amusing themselves to death. It is easy to be overly negative and agree that the plethora of personal opinion on the internet undermines the authority of the expert, supports deliberate scaremongering, spreads conspiracy theories and is dumbing down society, but it is important to remember that the internet still has the revolutionary potential to offer a voice to those who would otherwise be silenced. Ensuring these voices are listened to is an essential social priority.

Digital footprints

So far in this chapter we have looked at the permanence of our digital footprints, in particular with regard to social media, but there are other implications attached to our online activities and behaviours. Google have built their entire search industry around the philosophy of focusing on the user in the belief that all else will follow (Auletta, 2009). To do this effectively, every time the Google search engine is used records are kept of all websites visited in order to store and match the statistics with paid-for advertising content. Since the end of 2009, Google has been personalising its individual search results based on previous internet activity. As a result no two researchers looking at the same topic will receive the same set of results. All the time search engines are becoming more powerful and exacting. Not only are they faster and more accurate than ever before, they now incorporate semantic technology. This means digital relationships are made between different digital content; not only is this used to try and align your research results more with your own previous online history but also it enables retail companies to match like with like in the hope of encouraging visitors to buy something they might not have intended to buy when they visited their website. Semantic marketing is a powerful selling technique offering what appears to be a personalised shopping experience; one where all that is needed is a few clicks to make a financial transaction. One of the disadvantages of internet shopping is the multiple instances where our personal and financial details are entered and stored in vast digital databases; the more we shop online the more we increase the risk of becoming a victim of cybercrime.

Cybercrime

Travelling between websites on the internet is rarely a case of straight line connections between one and the other as you might expect. Instead, data is transferred through circuitous digital routes via a number of intermediary computer systems and these indirect courses increase the risk of information being copied. It is not unknown for an intermediary computer to be set up with a false identity and pretend to be the intended destination in order to siphon off personal details. Cybercrime describes the multiple ways in which digital criminals specialise in the transfer of confidential information, such as passwords, credit card numbers or online banking details. Internet fraud ranges from easy to spot scams to more sophisticated attempts to steal identities or con people out of money. Unfortunately it is often those who are the most trusting who see an online offer or a request for help as authentic without questioning it more deeply. It is important to advise all internet users to be suspicious, in particular if they get an email which asks for personal details, and always to remember that if an online offer sounds as if it is too good to be true then it very probably is. There are a number of different examples of Cybercrime and we will look at some of the most common ones in more detail.

Phishing

Phishing describes attempts to persuade users to give away personal information such as a password or Personal Identity Number (PIN) for an online banking account, or for some other registered payment system such as PayPal or Amazon. Phishing emails can copy bank or company logos and colour schemes in an attempt to make them look genuine and on the surface can often appear to be convincing. These emails may contain messages informing the recipient they have won a lottery or they might appeal for money for the victims of a national disaster. It is always safe to assume that any email which requests personal details is a scam as official companies will never do this. If there is any doubt it is better to advise users to contact the company concerned and request verification rather than respond to the email. Banks in particular will never ask customers to enter a password or any other sensitive information by clicking on a link or visiting a website. Phishing emails are sent out at random in the hope of reaching a live email address of a customer, either with an account at the bank being targeted, or who will be persuaded to send money. These scams should always be reported either by forwarding them to the ISP or to Bank Safe Online at www.banksafeonline.org.uk which is a service company providing expertise to the UK payments industry.

For more information about protecting yourself from online crime visit Get Safe Online at http://www.getsafeonline.org. This is a joint initiative between the UK Government, law enforcement, leading businesses and the public sector to ensure safety online with information about anti-virus software and anti-theft advice designed to ensure digital criminals are unable to take advantage of individual users.

Identity fraud

Identity fraud is not limited to the internet; being careless with personal offline documentation can lead to someone getting hold of information and using it dishonestly, for example claiming a credit card or setting up a bank loan. However, it is much easier to become the victim of identity fraud online and users need to be extra vigilant when keying in personal information such as credit card details and be careful which companies they use. There is nothing to stop anyone from setting up a website with an online payment system so it is good advice to shop only with recognised companies. All reputable organisations will have a privacy policy which should be read to ensure they guarantee not to pass on personal details. Some companies will pass these on by default or put your default agreement in the small print on registration, so it is worth advising users to seek these out in case they need to find the relevant form on the website and uncheck the agreement box. Another way of defeating identity fraud is to take care with passwords used, in particular on sites which contain credit card or other personal details. Combinations of letters and numbers are usually harder for password hacking software to detect; however, the more complex the password system devised, the more difficult it can be to remember which password belongs to which website. There is no easy answer to this conundrum but the time invested in creating a personal password system which is memorable to the individual while difficult for anyone else to understand will always be time well spent.

The websites below provide further information on internet identity fraud.

www.identitytheft.org.uk contains help for individuals to best protect themselves online.

www.direct.gov.uk contains practical advice and information about how to avoid being a victim of online fraud.

---

*ACTIVITY **1.1** STRONG PASSWORDS*

Spend a few minutes thinking about the passwords you use to access different sites on the internet. How do you manage your online passwords? Do you have separate ones for different accounts or do you use the same password for everything? Remembering all your individual passwords can be a challenge. Do you have them all written down on a piece of paper or stored in a file on your computer? Where do you keep the password list or what is your password file called?

COMMENT

Passwords are the first line of defence against cybercriminals. Software programs will try every word in the dictionary as well as random combinations of letters to try and hack into accounts. The most common passwords include the word Password and the letter combination 12345678 so avoid using these. Strong passwords contain a combination of letters, numbers and keyboard symbols. Do not use your name or any commonly known information, have a unique password for banking and change passwords regularly. Remember, no one will ever ask you for your password; if they do, get in touch with the alleged company concerned.

Spam

Spam is the name given to unsolicited emails which advertise illegal products or have attachments which contain viruses designed to damage your computer. A virus program is deliberately malicious software which can destroy information on the hard drive or attach itself to addresses in a contact list and target them all in the same way. Virus links are commonly sent out through Spam so these should be treated the same as Phishing emails; ignore and delete them. Advise users never to open an attachment on an email unless the sender is known and the authenticity of the attachment can be guaranteed. Some Spam emails may include threats or intimidating language designed to make the user feel obliged to respond to requests. Chain emails asking the user to pass on content to other people can also contain veiled threats or promises of extreme good fortune. It is always safe to ignore these types of communication; if the sender is unknown then the email should be treated with suspicion and deleted.

It is illegal to send out unsolicited marketing email unless the user has given permission; this is another reason for checking the small print when registering personal details online because signing up to a website or service often involves signing up for advertising emails from that company. The Information Commissioner's Office (ICO) at www.ico.gov.uk is a UK independent authority set up to uphold information rights in the public interest. The ICO offers help and advice to individuals to help prevent unwanted spam email.

Viruses

The harmful effect of digital viruses should never be underestimated. Viruses are small, malicious computer programs deliberately written to infiltrate the recipient computer. Often referred to as Worms or Trojans, once a virus manages to infect a computer it can easily be spread from one machine to the next. Viruses may attach themselves to emails, be hidden inside websites when you visit them or disguise themselves as something which seems innocent such as a picture or a special offer. Many viruses will prevent your computer from working efficiently or damage the information you have stored on it. This can be expensive to fix and frequently involves a processes called Ghosting, where all the disk drives are stripped, with a loss of data which may have serious consequences if it has not been backed up. Other viruses are more sophisticated and deliberately scan your computer for personal information such as passwords or create a link to your online information for criminals to access and take control. Some viruses can exist without the user being aware of them, which is why care should be taken never to open an unknown attachment or click on a link from an unknown email address. Pop-up windows must be closed down using the operating system Task Manager function rather than the small cross in the top right-hand corner and correct use of up-to-date anti-virus security software is essential.

CASE STUDY

Never too late to learn

Yahmir's grandfather, Rahul, has attended a computer class for beginners at his local community centre. Rahul is impressed with the different things he can do online. He tells Yahmir he wants to buy a computer so he can access the internet at home. Yahmir is concerned about his grandfather being safe online. He tells him about the dangers

Continued

---

inherent in phishing and scams and how he needs to be careful not to get any viruses. Rahul is irritated with what he sees as Yahmir's negativity. He thinks his grandson is trying to put him off being independent and managing a computer and exploring the internet on his own. However, Yahmir is genuinely worried that without knowing how to stay safe, his grandfather will make mistakes which might make him vulnerable to cyber-criminals. Rahul and Yahmir agree on a set of guidelines for online shopping. Rahul will check that the letters 'http' in the address bar have changed to 'https' as this signifies it is a secure site. He will look for the small yellow padlock in the browser tool bar, as this also signifies safety, and check that the address bar changes colour, which is an extended validation feature verifying a genuine site. Yahmir advises his grandfather not to open any email attachments or click a link in an email if he doesn't recognise the sender. Yahmir then buys and installs an internet security program and shows his grandfather how it works. For someone starting to use a computer for the first time there is a lot to learn about staying safe online but it is better to understand the dangers and learn how to protect yourself and your personal data rather than risk any potentially expensive errors.

Whistle-blowing and WikiLeaks

A whistle-blower is a person who tells the public or someone in authority about alleged dishonest or illegal activities occurring in a public or private organisation or company. Activities might be criminal or fraudulent, violate health and safety or be evidence of corruption. The potential for anonymity on the internet has made whistle-blowing easier. In 2006 the internet site called WikiLeaks started publishing private, secret and classified information from anonymous news sources, news leaks and whistle-blowers. By the end of 2010 WikiLeaks had published more than 70,000 classified US military files on the conflict in Afghanistan and a further 250,000 confidential government documents on Iraq. Opinions became divided between viewing whistle-blowing as being socially responsible or a breach of security. On the one side, the US government claimed the publication of embassy cables put the lives of diplomats and intelligence professionals at risk. On the other side, the leaks have been hailed as a positive step towards freedom of information and ensuring the public have a right to access official documents regardless of how sensitive they may be. At the time of writing the WikiLeaks site has been closed down but the use of the internet for whistle-blowing is likely to continue.

As social workers you will be working with people who are on the peripheries of society, through age, disability or incapacity, and may witness instances where people tasked to provide care do not appear regulated or well supervised. The GSCC Code of Practice requires the bringing to the attention of employers, or the appropriate authority resource, any operational difficulties that might get in the way of the delivery of safe care, so there is a moral imperative to raise concerns, and a contractual requirement to do so. However, fear of victimisation is often cited as the reason for individuals failing to speak out (Rodie, 2009; Hunter, 2009; Calcraft, 2007). Public Concern at Work is an independent authority with information on public interest whistle-blowing. They offer free advice to people with whistle-blowing dilemmas on their website at www.pcaw.co.uk and you might want to add this address to your list of useful websites.

Freedom of speech on the internet

Whistle-blowing online is possible because the internet supports freedom of speech. The capacity for censorship was never built into its structures and although there are countries where governments exercise control through the filtering and blocking of unwanted information, the free and open nature of the major part of the internet makes it difficult to keep secrets. Twitter is an example of a social media program which has gained a reputation for exercising freedom of speech outside of the law. It has become a primary channel for information during wars, where local internet connections have been restricted, and there have been several occasions in the UK where Tweeters have directly challenged injunctions put in place to prevent certain information being made public. Twitter has shown how it can be impossible to control what is said online. When protected information cannot legally be disclosed in the UK media, but can be made available on Twitter and accessed by people in the UK, then it makes it difficult for courts to impose sanctions. The right to freedom of speech is recognised as a human right under Article 19 of the Universal Declaration of Human Rights. In practice, however, the right to freedom of speech is commonly subject to limitations such as those that prohibit incitement to acts of hate or terrorism. While the internet's potential for universal access can be compromised politically by individual governments, limitations on individual use remain difficult to impose and legislate for. This makes it almost impossible to prevent freedom of use and expression. For more information about freedom of speech go to the websites below:

Universal Declaration of Human Rights at www.un.org and search for declaration of human rights;

UK government law on freedom of speech at www.legislation.gov.uk and search for race and religious hatred.

Internet gaming

The power of anytime anywhere online connectivity has the potential to magnify offline behaviours and the media frequently contain stories about individual addiction to digital practices, for example gambling. Problems created by online gambling addiction are examined more closely in Chapter 5. It is not only gambling which can create addictive behaviour patterns; addiction to internet gaming has also been cited as a cause for concern. Online gaming enables players to play virtually with other people via massively multiplayer online role-playing games (MMORPGs). MMORPGs originated from Dungeons and Dragons, a role-playing game played on pen and paper in the 1970s, and today they frequently consist of networks of players who achieve goals, go on missions, and reach high scores in 3D digital fantasy worlds. Computers and the internet have revolutionised these early role-playing games and some of the most popular include *World of Warcraft*, *Warhammer* and *Runescape*. Gaming addicts can spend progressively more time online playing games and neglecting important tasks such as school, work and other social activities. Online gambling support groups like www.gamcare.org.uk offer support for gaming addicts, as do Gamers Anonymous at www.olganon.org.

You may already have spotted the contradiction inherent in internet-based support for online addictions: the need to use the same environment that fostered the original problem. This dichotomy is typical of the dual nature of the internet which on the one hand supports potentially negative behaviour and on the other attempts to neutralise the effects. There is no easy answer to these conundrums and the issue lies at the tip of the dark side of the internet where some of the more difficult aspects of human behaviour can be manifested and exploited.

Internet pornography

The internet has not invented pornography but it has contributed to an increased amount of criminal activity including the creation, distribution and sharing of illegal online pornographic content. The subject of pornography raises a host of moral and political issues including trade regulation, users' privacy, and individual rights. In the UK there is regulation of other media channels such as television, cinema, high street advertising hoardings and content on newsagent shelves in order to prevent children seeing inappropriate images. In addition mobile phone companies are able to restrict access to adult material. So far the calls for ISPs to regulate the distribution of content on the internet have run contrary to the internet philosophy of neutrality. The EU Kids Online survey (Livingstone, et al., 2010) looks at the effects of accidental exposure to offensive images and suggests the advantages of internet access equals and in places outweighs the risks. The report concludes that the key focus should be on appropriate education and parental controls as these are important sources of advice and should offer coping tools where children inadvertently encounter upsetting content.

The relationship between online pornography, fantasy and real-world actions has not been definitively established. However, there are suggestions of a causal link between access to extreme online images and cases of sexual abuse and that the internet may be catalysing this relationship between thinking and doing.

> *The virtual space, therefore, may play an important role in supporting and catalysing the link between thinking and doing through the provision of a third tier in an individual's 'own world'. This tier can be viewed as the step between pure fantasy and reality, but one which can reinforce, manipulate and alter the transition from thinking into doing.*

> (Wilson and Jones, 2008, p4)

The internet offers a virtual space free from restrictions and this may be used inappropriately, resulting in boundaries between virtual and real worlds becoming blurred. The degree to which this is a cause for public concern has not yet been fully established but any direct links will be as much related to individual lives and circumstances as to what is seen and done online; the internet is more likely to be exacerbating existing behaviour traits than creating them.

The internet: A social mirror

In 2010 Facebook users were encouraged to change their profile to a cartoon character in a campaign to raise awareness against child abuse. The NSPCC allegedly backed the campaign but although they publicly supported it, they claimed not to know its origin. People were divided on whether this was a genuine attempt to raise awareness of child abuse or a hoax instigated by a paedophile ring trying to entice children to add cartoon characters as their friends. The furore which surrounded this followed the case in 2009 of the nursery worker Vanessa George, who was committed on seven charges of child abuse and six of taking indecent photographs of children in her care, reigniting fears that the internet was supporting and encouraging child sexual abuse. In this case George, along with Angela Allen and Colin Blanchard, formed a trio of Facebook 'friends' who met online and exchanged indecent messages and images. Cases like this, which include Facebook sites being set up in response to high-profile media crimes such as those relating to Ian Huntley and the death of Baby Peter, can result in Facebook becoming the focus for an outpouring of public hatred against the perpetrators. It seems inevitable that for every instance where the internet is used to support positive, humanistic activities, there will be others where it attracts negative and antagonistic interaction.

Concern is frequently expressed by the media over websites set up with the aim of supporting harmful conditions or behaviour such as eating disorders or cutting. Rather than offering helpful advice, some sites do appear to encourage sufferers of conditions such as anorexia and bulimia or who self-harm. Authoritative medical websites are a useful source of information about personal conditions but they can enhance hypochondria by creating unnecessary worry and concern. There are multiple examples of the duality of the internet for harming or healing and little doubt that it mirrors both the positive and negative aspects of human endeavours. How much these actions are exacerbated by its capacity for 24/7 access and anonymity remains an open debate.

Positive aspects to a digital society

However much this chapter has seemed full of doom and gloom, it is not all bad news! The internet offers incredible opportunities for democratic access to information and communication and its affordances are the key drivers in creating and sustaining an increasingly digital society with enormous impact on daily life. We have changed the way in which we communicate, learn, shop and access entertainment. People send and receive information in seconds rather than days or weeks; barriers to doing business or engaging in collaborative research across continents have been reduced and families use email and instant messaging facilities such as MSN and Skype to keep in touch in a way that has never before been possible. As a research and learning tool, the internet hosts a vast library of data where finding information can be as simple as entering a few words into a search engine, with knowledge being gained in minutes rather than hours or days. The rapid transfer of data means that people can travel less, with more sustainable online contact being maintained as easily via a computer screen as via a meeting table in the real world.

There are few aspects of life in the twenty-first century which have not been affected by the internet and in this chapter we have been investigating the social impact of digital ways of working. It may seem that at times the emphasis has been unnecessarily negative but new users approaching the internet for the first time do need to know about online safety. Not all content is appropriate for all people and there are real risks involved in the careless management of personal information, in particular for people unfamiliar with digital environments. The internet is an amazing place. It offers opportunities for communication unfettered by time and distance and access to a mass of information which would have been unimaginable just a decade ago. There are great benefits to be had from the vast range of digital resources and the flexibility of their distribution and access. However, there is also the need to be aware that for all its affordances, the internet and the world wide web remain mirrors of our society, with all its weaknesses as well as all its strengths, and for sections of the population access to these new digital worlds is still being denied.

CHAPTER SUMMARY

- The internet is a free and open environment with an absence of controls over content. This has resulted in a virtual mirroring of the positive and negative aspects of society. The philosophy of altruism which was the basis of the internet has been challenged by a capitalist economy, resulting in internet users themselves becoming digital commodities. Profiles of digital travels are stored and used to target future advertising while our digital footprints are permanent, meaning content posted carelessly or in haste is difficult to control or erase.

- Digital information and communication technologies are not neutral; they are socially shaped and reflect the existing social and political environment in which they are designed and delivered. Current thinking supports educating users to stay safe online and take responsibility for their digital lives in the same way as they would take responsibility for their non-digital ones.

- Research suggests digital exclusion is related to existing categories of social exclusion with potential implications for social work education and practice. Students and practitioners need to develop confidence and competence when working in digital environments while recognising the parameters of digital access and the effect of exclusion in an increasingly digital society.

FURTHER READING

Carr, N (2010) *The shallows: What the internet is doing to our brains*. New York: Norton and Co.

A critical examination of the effect of the internet on the brain and the way in which information is processed. While acknowledging the benefits of digital access to knowledge, Carr raises interesting questions about society's relationship with the internet and where it might be heading.

Keen, A (2007) *The cult of the amateur: How today's internet is killing our culture and assaulting our economy*. London: Nicholas Brealey Publishing.

A critique of an internet society which suggests the user-generated content nature of Web 2.0 is damaging traditional conceptions of the professional as the source of expertise. Instead, the populist nature of the internet is prioritising the voices of the novice and the amateur.

Rafferty, J and Steyaert, J (2007) Social work in a digital society. In Lymbery, M and Postle, K (eds) *Social work: A companion to learning*. London: Sage.

An exploration of how new information and communications technologies have impacted on society and irretrievably altered the nature of the social world, which now needs to be reconceptualised if social work practitioners are to manage effectively within a digital society.

Steyaert, J and Gould, N (2009) Social work and the changing face of the digital divide. *British Journal of Social Work*, 39(4), 740–53.

Exploring the concept of the digital divide in relation to social exclusion and asking if the divide is narrowing or getting wider. The implications of digital divides for the social work profession are examined in the light of divides being less about access and more about the ways in which that access is used.

Chapter 2

Contemporary digital policy and social work practice

Introduction

Public services in our society are increasingly being offered digitally and the UK government is committed to providing digital-by-default services. We have moved rapidly from an era in which we interacted with government only via traditional mechanisms (telephone, letter or face-to-face contact) to a state in which the ambition is for digital technology to provide the means by which all citizens will be able to interact with government when and where they choose, and in which there will be constant, round-the-clock accessibility, at home, at work and on the move. This chapter will examine the development of digital services in the UK using a number of well-known or pertinent examples from a variety of public services. You may well have experienced a range of online government services yourself: applications for student loans, or for a tax disc for your car, for example. From such experiences you may have made a judgement about the general effectiveness of online services and public systems which rely on digital technologies. In this chapter we will examine some of the problems that can and frequently have beset large digital technology programmes associated with government, as well as examples of good practice and good outcomes. The drivers for the push for digital-by-default services in terms of both policy and the development and availability of technology will be examined. The chapter will also examine the implications of this development in terms of one of the main themes of the book; that of digital divides. In a digital-by-default era will services also be accessible by default? Or will those without access to all aspects of digital services receive a second-class or residual service and become a digital underclass? Those without access might include older people, users of assistive technologies, those living in rural areas without connections, the unemployed and speakers of other languages. These are groups who also tend to face other kinds of social exclusion and, it should be noted, feature heavily in the caseloads of social workers. We will consider how those policies which emphasise digital access intertwine with other contemporary social policies such as personalisation; highlight some relevant legal developments; and consider some of the specific implications of all of these developments in policy and law for the social care sector.

Technology and government policy

At the end of 2010 a report suggested that shifting 50 per cent of the contacts that people have with public services to digital channels, meaning largely the internet, could save the government over two billion pounds a year (Lane Fox, 2010a). An administration searching for huge savings in the cost of the state was persuaded and announced the ambition of providing all government services as digital by default.

The policy of governments in the UK and elsewhere has, for several decades, been following a trajectory towards providing services online. In the mid 1990s governments in various countries became excited that it might be possible to 'square the circle' and produce 'better government that costs less' in the words of a US review of the period, which highlighted the potential of digital technologies to modernise and make government both more efficient and more responsive to the needs of citizens (Office of the Vice President, 1993). In the UK, the Conservative government of John Major produced a significant Green Paper in 1996 which examined the potential for using computers and the internet to deliver government and make it more efficient (Cabinet Office Central IT Unit, 1996). This was followed by a flurry of policymaking by the New Labour government headed by Tony Blair, who was convinced that the impact of technology was one of the most significant aspects of the age in which he was governing and suggested that the economic and social changes in train were as fundamental as the shift from agrarian to industrial production (Blair, 1999). The Blair government produced a White Paper called Modernising Government which revealed the scale of the ambition for moving government services online. Targets were set for the implementation of what was referred to as e-government. Initially these were 25 per cent by 2002 and 100 per cent by 2008. This 100 per cent was later brought forward to 2005 (Hudson, 2002).

Gordon Brown, as Chancellor of the Exchequer, made a number of high-profile speeches about the need to reposition the British economy as one which was in the centre of the digital revolution and where significant numbers of high-tech, high-skill jobs could be created. It seemed clear to many policymakers that to participate in the new globalised and technological economy, and to gain well-paid employment, a certain level of competency and skill with digital technologies was becoming more and more necessary. Tony Blair, in his 1999 Beveridge lecture, suggested that globalisation has placed a premium on workers with the skills and knowledge to adapt to advancing technology (Blair, 1999, p3).

It can be seen that there were several different drivers of the government's seeming enthusiasm for getting everybody and everything online. Certainly policymakers were aware that a sound economic future required a workforce and an infrastructure of high skill and high tech. At the same time, faced with inexorable rises in the costs of public services, and buoyed by the promises of significant efficiencies and cost savings, the drive towards Electronic Delivery of Services (EDS) gathered new momentum.

Technology, policy and inclusion

While governments are always attracted to measures which appear to promise significant cost savings, New Labour also viewed the development of digital technologies as an opportunity to genuinely improve the quality of public services and redefine the way in which the public interacted with government. This was a government which talked a lot about social exclusion and there was awareness among New Labour policymakers of the danger of reinforcing existing exclusions in the push to make greater use of digital technologies in many aspects of public life. To address the danger of these new forms of exclusion developing, the New Labour government set up a policy action team to specifically address the 'digital divide' (Department for Trade and Industry, 2000). One of Tony Blair's key aims for information-age government was for internet access to be universal and he took active steps to ensure that this was achieved. Practical examples of schemes that followed from this included installing refurbished computers in the homes of 100,000 socially excluded families and setting up the UK Online Centres.

CASE STUDY

UK Online Centres

UK Online Centres were a product of a policy initiative aimed at reducing digital divides (DTI 2000). The aim was to develop a widespread network of community-based facilities which would offer free or low-cost access to the internet, along with advice and training. There are 6,000 such facilities in the UK and it is estimated that 70 per cent of users of these centres have at least one indicator of social disadvantage (UK Online Centres, 2010). While half of the users of these centres have no formal qualifications when first attending, 40 per cent go on to paid or voluntary work or formal learning (UK Online Centres, 2010). The centres also champion the use of MyGuide, a service which morphed in October 2011 into Go On at www.go-on.co.uk. This service provides a free email account and web access. The site provides access to a range of courses and useful resources and aims to raise awareness of a range of online government services including health and welfare sites such as NHS choices.

Continued

As well as the work done by the UK Online Centres to reduce digital divides there are a number of organisations which have been active in improving the use and accessibility of technology for people with disabilities. AbilityNet at www.abilitynet.org.uk are one of the leading authorities on issues relating to disability and the use of digital technologies. Their slogan is 'Adapting Technology, Changing Lives' and they provide detailed advice on adapting computers and offer a range of training courses designed to raise awareness of issues around digital inclusion.

ACTIVITY **2.1** *ABILITYNET*

Visit the AbilityNet website at www.abilitynet.org.uk. You should see on the home page a heading which says 'Exploring AAC'. Click on this link, which takes you to a website for Augmentative and Alternative Communication. Explore the site both with and without speech enabled. You will see headings for buttons, paper overlays, dynamic devices, AAC software, text only, physical access and 'my kit' choices. Explore each of these areas for detailed information about a range of technologies which can assist with communication.

COMMENT

On the AbilityNet website you will note a wide range of different technologies and approaches for assisting communication. Not all involve digital technologies but many do and they make it possible to improve the abilities of people with a range of impairments to communicate more effectively. There is also a wide range in the cost of these technologies and some may remain out of reach for those who might benefit most from their use.

The initiatives described above made only partial inroads into the problem and significant digital divides remained in Britain in the early part of the new millennium. By 2008 a new policy to tackle the issue was produced. This was the Delivering Digital Inclusion Action Plan, a brainchild of the Department for Culture, Media and Sport (DCMS, 2008) and outlined the role of digital champions and digital mentors. The Minister for Digital Inclusion at the time recognised the need for action: *Inequality in the use and application of digital technologies is a new driver of social exclusion in the 21st century, which risks accelerating existing social divides and creating new ones. Digital exclusion is a symptom of wider exclusion, but also a cause* (Murphy, 2008, p4).

Specific outcomes from this policy included the appointment of a Digital Champion to drive forward the efforts to get more of the excluded to be included.

Race Online 2012

Martha Lane Fox, a businesswoman who developed a successful online business at www. lastminute.com was appointed as the Digital Champion for the nation. She set up Race Online 2012, an independent campaign with the aim of getting as much of the nation as possible online in time for the London Olympics in 2012. The campaign enlisted 100,000 'digital champions' to try to motivate and support the significant minority of the population who were not yet online to do so. The size of that minority was estimated at ten million, or one in five of the population, at the start of the campaign (Lane Fox, 2010a). At the time of writing this initiative had succeeded in helping more than a million people to get online. It also had the ear of government. The Cabinet Minister Francis Maude said at the time that he was minded to accept the recommendations of the 2010 manifesto in their entirety (Maude, 2010).

The global economic crisis, which was followed by the election of the coalition government in England, and a massive focus on reducing public debt, seems to have been followed by a widespread perception that the major driver for public policy must be reducing cost to the public purse. In this climate issues of accessibility and inclusion have been heard about less. Certainly there can be significant costs attached to providing training and hardware and software for all disadvantaged groups to access technology. In a time of significant cuts to public expenditure, programmes which demonstrated a good track record of improving digital inclusion were cut back. Economic arguments in support of severe austerity followed the line that it is necessary to reduce public debt quickly in order to stimulate growth. Yet there is sound evidence to suggest that the provision of digital access can lead to significant cost benefits and actually be a driver of growth. A European Commission report of 2007 estimated *If all of the then current EU policy targets on digital inclusion were met, economic growth in Europe could be boosted by €85 billion in the next five years* (European Commission, 2007, p96).

The coalition government did recognise this at some level and continued support for Race Online 2012, though funding was lost for some of the local projects that Race Online 2012 had identified as the best means of tackling digital exclusion.

Digital issues and the law

In your social work study programme you will cover a number of aspects of the law. You will learn about statutes relating to children and families, adult social care, equalities, mental health, and others. It is often the case that the law provides the driver for local authorities and social workers to get involved and to take action in relation to a particular issue. With respect to digital issues there are several aspects of the law which are worth considering, in terms of both government policy and the role of local authorities and social workers.

Perhaps one clear measure of the strength of will behind government policy is the willingness to enshrine it in legislation. While this is not always necessary or appropriate it is noteworthy that although some European countries are enshrining rights of digital access (for example Finland which enshrined a legal right to broadband in 2009), the current UK government has moved away from this and prefers a voluntary target of universal fast broadband services being available across the nation by 2012.

Some have argued that rather than enabling access, legislation in the UK actually moved in the opposite direction with the passing of the Digital Economy Act in 2010. One of its main aims was to tackle illegal sharing of digital materials, such as downloading music. Within the act there are provisions to remove internet access for those who contravene it. Such was the concern about this provision that the United Nations Human Rights Council issued a statement expressing deep concern over the potential for *centralised control over internet usage*, suggesting that cutting off internet usage in response to violation of intellectual copyright was disproportionate and a violation of the international covenant on civil and political rights (La Rue, 2011, p22). It has also been admitted that the costs of policing and enforcing the Digital Economy Act may be passed on to consumers and lead to low-income users being priced out of internet access. At the time of writing a significant campaign to repeal the Digital Economy Act had not been successful, though some concessions were made on the issue of removing internet access for individuals. Given the continuing policy emphasis on getting everyone online and doing government business online, it does seem perverse that the activities of a few transgressors who illegally download music and films might lead to increasing digital exclusion and the inability of large numbers of citizens to access what are now considered basic services such as applying for a car road tax licence or banking online. We are in danger of engineering a situation which Tambini warned about a decade ago; one in which *Electronic service delivery will look increasingly illegitimate as citizens that have paid for those services will have no access to them* (Tambini, 2001, p12).

The Chronically Sick and Disabled Persons Act 1970

Social work has a long tradition of providing and arranging for aids and adaptations for people with a range of impairments. The Chronically Sick and Disabled Persons Act of 1970 made it a legal duty for local authorities to do so and this became an important function of social services departments. The range of assistive devices and technologies which are available has increased exponentially since then. The kinds of aids and adaptations that might help a person to take part in activities that the rest of society take for granted are increasingly linked to digital devices and there are now many technologies which support a diversity of ways of using computers and accessing the internet. Such assistive technologies include but are not limited to alternatives to a computer mouse, such as touch-screen sensors; alternatives to a keyboard, such as eye-operated systems; and speech-recognition software. Some of these will be looked at in more detail later in this chapter and in other parts of the book. Although it is not the only way in which social workers can support those with impairments, arranging for the provision of suitable assistive technologies remains a significant means by which a social worker can empower a service user towards the maintenance of or increase in independence.

Equality Act 2010

This law replaced or updated most provisions of the Disability Discrimination Act (DDA) 1995. You may be aware that the DDA provided legal rights for people in relation to education, employment and the provision of goods and services. The act states that any provider of goods or services must make reasonable adjustments when there are barriers to accessing those goods or services for those with disabilities. Guidance from the Equality and Human Rights Commission (EHRC) suggests that such reasonable adjustments include providing extra equipment or removal of physical barriers to enable access. The EHRC can take action in relation to online services including helping to bring cases under the Equalities Act and closing down websites. This action has not yet been taken but it is not ruled out by the Commission. The lack of legal action to date is somewhat surprising given the number of websites which remain inaccessible to many. The last major survey of public websites was undertaken in 2004 by the Disability Rights Commission (DRC). They found that of 1,000 UK website home pages fewer than one in five met the most basic accessibility requirements, meaning that one or more disabled groups would find the majority of all websites difficult to use. The DRC document was an important landmark in the move towards creating a digitally inclusive society. As well as highlighting the inaccessibility of many public websites, it made a series of recommendations, two of which have particular relevance to the themes of this book:

- Recommendation 12: in line with its commitment to 'bridge the digital divide', the Government should provide the funding required to enable access to appropriate assistive technology for all those who need it, and to promote its better use (2004, p40).

- Recommendation 13: existing health, social and rehabilitation services with responsibility for assessing their clients' needs for physical aids attend, and respond, to the Web accessibility needs of disabled people (2004, p4).

While you are on placement and practice it will be worth looking for evidence for the implementation of these recommendations. In many cases you will find barriers to digital access still exist. There is more information about digital exclusion in Chapter 3.

Public services go digital
HMRC

Her Majesty's Revenue and Customs service was one of the first government services to provide an online face. Once launched, the online system for submitting self-assessment tax returns quickly became popular and now almost seven million people use this rather than the paper-based version (some 78 per cent of the total). While there have been some high-profile problems, including the loss of child benefit data, and incorrect tax demands being sent to people, this large government department does a lot of its business efficiently online with over a billion computer transactions processed and 450 million emails sent each year. HMRC services are accessed via the portal to all online government services, known as Directgov at www.direct.gov.uk.

CASE STUDY

The Directgov website
In September 2007 the Directgov website at www.direct.gov.uk received visitor number 100 million (Central Office of Information, 2007). Since being established in 2004, to replace the previous UK Online Portal, this site has developed to a point at which it now receives over 20 million hits a month from eight million different users (Directgov, 2009). The site is designed both as a central repository of information and as a platform for completing transactions with the government. You may have used the site yourself to find out about student finance, to apply for a TV licence, passport, or driving licence, to register to vote or to complete an online self-assessment tax return.

Continued

CASE STUDY *continued*

In keeping with the drive to make government technology platforms more visible and interactive and to make such interaction easier for citizens, Directgov has developed a presence on social media sites including Facebook, Twitter and YouTube; a mobile phone platform and availability via digital TV with a presence on Freeview, Sky and Virgin channels. Significant efforts have been made to make the online site more accessible and Directgov now claims to be accessible to all citizens, whether or not they have any disabilities. It is compatible with screen-reading software and can be navigated using only a keyboard for those who are unable to use a mouse.

Directgov has attracted a range of criticisms. A well-publicised alternative website called Directionless was set up to illustrate the point that much of the information provided at the Directgov website could be found directly and quickly by anyone using simple Google searches. In April 2010, the site introduced a feedback and comment facility. The bottom of every page of the site now offers users a chance to rate the usefulness of the information provided. In the year after it was introduced the site received 1.5 million ratings. Half of all users found the site very useful and the percentage finding it 'not at all useful' had dropped from 22 per cent to 16 per cent after ten months of feedback and responses.

Partly in response to criticisms of the site, and also in response to the recommendations of Martha Lane Fox (which were touched on earlier), the government set up a new experimental public interface in 2011 called Alpha at www.alpha.gov.uk. Alpha was designed to use more effective search technology and to provide an easier-to-use interface for public services.

ACTIVITY **2.2** ACCESSIBLE ONLINE CONTENT

Go to the Directgov website at www.direct.gov.uk. At the top of each page, on the right-hand side, there is the heading 'Accessibility'. Click on this. Read the information which is provided about the accessibility of the site and listen to the audio recording which discusses this issue.

COMMENT

The Directgov website has better accessibility than many others. Compatibility with World Wide Web Consortium's (W3C) Web Content Accessibility Guidelines is a standard to look out for, which the Directgov site achieves. These guidelines have been developed by a group of people who have come together to develop international standards for the accessibility of the web. The consortium is currently chaired by the inventor of the world wide web, Tim Berners-Lee, a man who from the start advocated full accessibility standards. Also look out for compatibility with screen-reading software, which provides the facility for 'reading' what appears on the screen and then converting it to speech or other formats such as Braille.

Housing

Housing provides an exemplar which highlights a number of the major issues with regard to the move towards digital policies and practices which we wish to draw to your attention. These include maintaining and increasing independence (telecare and specialist housing design), consumer choice and personalisation (choice-based letting), digital exclusion (social housing) and the effects of various government policies.

Social housing

Over 18 per cent of all households in the UK live in social housing, which is defined as *affordable housing which is rented out by social landlords* (Shelter, 2009, p2). Social landlords are non-commercial bodies, which generally means a local authority or a housing association. It is clear that vulnerable groups are concentrated in social housing; nearly a quarter of those aged over seventy-five and a quarter of ethnic minority households for example (Shelter, 2009, pp4–6). More pertinent to this discussion is the fact that over two-thirds of people who live in social housing are not online, which is one-third of the digitally excluded adults in the UK (Social Housing Providers and Digital Inclusion Strategy Group, 2010). This means that social housing could provide a particular focus and target for initiatives to improve access and training for the digitally excluded. Social housing settings are often the first point of contact between a person and official public services, and may provide the first point at which social problems are identified. There are a number of case studies highlighting the potential for social landlords to provide training and motivation to residents in relation to technology, and also to provide technology-based solutions to identified problems. Examples include: online tenant forums; reporting of repairs and maintenance problems via interactive TVs, mobiles or computers; the provision of recycled computers to residents; free wireless internet access; rent packages which include broadband; and close links to training providers such as UK Online Centres. The National Housing Federation has argued strongly that taking responsibility for digital inclusion is a key aspect of their work to support the social welfare of residents. Two further striking statistics highlight the importance of this issue. First, 60 per cent of those in social housing are not in employment. While half of this number are retired the remainder are of working age. Second, 90 per cent of new jobs now require internet skills (Race Online 2012, 2011a, p30). One of the key recommendations made in the Manifesto for a Networked Nation is that *Social housing and residential care home providers should provide internet access and some ongoing support as a basic utility for their residents* (Race Online 2012, 2011a, p57).

Specialist housing for older people

Since 2004 the Department of Health and Homes and Communities Agency have allocated some £800 million in capital grant funding to local authorities and their housing partners to invest in specialist housing for older people. We are all aware that people are living longer and that the overall profile of the population is an ageing one. There is simply a bigger proportion of the population in older age groups and with ageing comes an increasing likelihood of disability. A number of evaluations have indicated that small investments in the use of technology in people's homes can lead to significant cost savings in both the health and social care fields and also to significant impacts on the ability of individuals to remain independent within their own homes. Despite this the provision of such technologies has remained patchy. As both social norms and the availability of technology have progressed, there has been an increasing emphasis on providing support for independent living for older people. This may mean that rather than enter a residential care home a person who cannot manage daily activities well enough to live alone and independently is offered sheltered accommodation or Extra Care Housing (ECH). The latter is aimed at maximising independence, to the extent that a person maintains their own front door, with on-site and 24-hour availability of suitable care. Extra Care Housing is increasingly being fitted as standard with some of the technologies which are classed under the heading of telecare and which we discuss in more detail in Chapter 3. Examples include sensors to detect motion and falls and alarm buttons which connect directly to a person in a control centre who can call a relative or a warden immediately to provide help.

The report from the all-party parliamentary group on housing and care for older people made a large number of recommendations in June 2011 (Porteus, 2011). A significant one was that the new Health and Well-being Boards, which local authorities have responsibility for, should include responsibilities relating to housing. The group were at pains to stress the links between health, social care and housing and the need to join up policy and practice in the three areas, in order to maximise independence and reduce unnecessary trauma and costs. Again this highlights the point that well-being and needs for social care may be intimately linked to a person's housing situation and local authorities and those who work for them need to think holistically about these issues. The report recognised the central importance of suitable housing in maintaining independence, health and well-being and preventing the need for institutional care. Evidence from a number of submissions to the authors of this report emphasised the growing place of assistive digital technologies as well as suitably designed houses, in this process of maintaining independence and helping people to 'live well at home'.

Choice-based letting

Choice-based lettings were brought in as a means of introducing an element of choice for those who apply for council or Housing Association homes. Initially developed in the Netherlands in the 1980s, the scheme was introduced to the UK in 2000 (Appleton and Molyneux, 2009). Based on a points and eligibility system, the scheme enables individuals to bid for available properties in their area. Information about the properties and the bidding system itself may be based on an online system, on written communication, or a combination of the two. Bearing in mind the Equality Act, authorities should take steps to make reasonable adjustments to ensure that their schemes, as well as the properties themselves, are accessible to all. Evaluations of the use of choice-based lettings by vulnerable groups suggest that on the whole they find it an equitable system compared to previous systems and like the transparency and amount of information available (Appleton and Molyneux, 2009). However, while researching for this book, the authors were made aware of settings in which moves to make the system predominantly an online one had led to exclusions for homeless people. A number of them described struggles to complete the online forms within the necessary timescales due to limited access to the internet at public places such as libraries or hostels.

Social work and housing

As a social worker you may work with many groups who have significant needs in relation to housing, including people with disabilities, with mental health problems, those subject to domestic violence and those leaving care. As Maslow's hierarchy of needs suggests, a secure roof over your head is a basic need and it is important to help people secure adequate and appropriate accommodation which meets their needs. Despite both often being situated within local authorities, housing and social work departments have not always communicated well together, but new ways of working and new opportunities are developing in this area. With the Personalisation Agenda, individuals are starting to be able to combine funding streams from social care and the Supporting People Programme into integrated budgets, and social workers will be involved in helping individuals secure housing-related support using their personal budgets rather than simply referring them to a housing department. Where they are involved in helping those with specific disadvantages to access suitable housing, social workers should discuss issues of digital access and help to advocate that housing should include the provision of secure and inexpensive internet access as well as access to suitable equipment and training to enable ease of use.

Health: NHS Direct

NHS Direct was created by the Department of Health in 1998 as a 24-hour advice service. Initially it was mainly a telephone-based service. Provision of the service via the internet gradually increased and in 2004 a digital TV service was also launched. NHS Direct, like many other public bodies, have significantly increased their use of social media. They established a presence on Twitter in 2008 and by 2011 had 9,000 followers with 12,000 on Facebook. A Tweet during the 2009 flu pandemic was seen by 40,000 people. Targeted adverts on Facebook were being discussed in 2011. There were suggestions, for example, that a person who talked on Facebook about suffering from flu might then see a targeted advert for the NHS Direct symptom checker. Further evidence that new technologies were proving popular for accessing NHS Direct information came when, within days of being released, their new app for the iPhone became the most popular free app at the iTunes store.

It is clear that certain groups in the population are keen to use not only websites but online social media to access and share information about health. However, we need to remember those who do not wish to or who cannot access the technology to use services in this way. In their business plan for 2011–2016, NHS Direct set out very clear goals for moving their core activity away from a central national telephone access service towards an emphasis on the remotely delivered and virtual services. This does not necessarily mean internet only. There is good evidence that some disadvantaged groups will use digital TV far more than the internet (Helsper et al., 2008) and NHS Direct is aware of this, has a successful track record in using this medium, and plans to continue developing this service. It is noteworthy that in their written statements about disability NHS Direct explicitly state that they support a social model of disability (NHS Direct 2008). If this is more than mere rhetoric then the organisation should continue to ensure that, they maintain a wide variety of platforms for accessing their services and that assistance is offered to ensure that, with or without the internet, and with or without disabilities, all citizens can access the same health information and services.

Also in 2011 the wider NHS produced an 'information revolution' strategy. At that time the chief technology officer announced that the policy of compelling all of the population to contact public services using digital channels, which seemed to be the thrust of government policy at the time, will not apply to health care. The emphasis was on using technology where appropriate to make a range of processes within the NHS more efficient but continuing to offer face-to-face and telephone contact where patients choose this. This was a tacit recognition that a significant minority of the population remain digitally excluded and that the NHS, which the British public have been committed to for 60 years as a universal and freely accessible service, needs to remain so.

Health services: Online therapy

As internet access has become more widely available and as technologies have developed, an increasing number of individuals are choosing or being advised to access forms of therapy online (Barak et al., 2008). The growth of literature on cybercounselling gives some indication of the mushrooming of this type of service (Liebert et al., 2006). Advantages of this development for service users include convenience, anonymity and lower costs. Indeed, studies suggest that the most frequent reasons for using internet counselling services are convenience, privacy and anonymity. It is well known that the largest percentage of human communication involves non-verbal aspects (Borg, 2006) and there is a danger that the absence of emotional cues and information from tone of voice, posture and so on, may lead to an impoverishment of the online therapeutic encounter. However, a number of techniques have been developed to provide additional information within online therapeutic encounters. For example, Mitchell and Murphy (1998) proposed a set of ideas which they labelled *presence techniques*, which allow for the communication of tone of voice and non-verbal information within text. Emotional bracketing, for example, allows for the provision of an emotional statement to follow in square brackets after the main statement. Alternatively the shorthand for emotions is sometimes used, for example :-) for smile, ;-) for wink, and :-(for sad.

Offering therapeutic input using online mechanisms clearly provides significant opportunities and advantages, as well as being constrained by several limitations. It is worth examining what the evidence actually says about such developments, particularly in comparison with traditional face-to-face therapeutic encounters. Many studies show that the therapeutic relationship or alliance is the key variable and carries more significance for outcomes than the mode or type of therapy being offered (Mitchell and Cormack, 1998). Studies indicate that such alliances are equally strong in online settings as those which develop in face-to-face settings (Cook and Doyle, 2002; Reynolds et al., 2006; Murphy et al., 2009). Indeed participants in such studies often reported specific and unique advantages of online settings. For example, online therapists rated their exchanges as deeper and smoother compared to face-to-face therapists (Reynolds et al., 2006, p164).

RESEARCH SUMMARY

Online therapy

A useful overview of the advantages, disadvantages and issues relating to online therapy can be gleaned from Murphy et al. *(2009). For an understanding of the data which relate to actual outcomes, the meta-analysis conducted by Barak* et al. *(2008) should be studied. These authors assessed and pooled data from 92 separate studies which involved almost 10,000 clients. Studies looked at internet-based psychotherapy. They concluded that internet-based therapy is on average as effective or nearly as effective as face-to-face therapy.*

The following year Murphy et al. *published in the* British Journal of Social Work *the findings of their research, which compared outcomes and client satisfaction from online therapy with face-to-face therapy (Murphy* et al., *2009, pp1–14). They concluded that online counselling can be as satisfying and impactful for clients as face-to-face counselling.*

Online gambling

As an example of the Janus-like or two-faced nature of the internet, gambling problems have been both significantly facilitated and multiplied by the explosion of online gambling opportunities and at the same time new opportunities have developed for offering help to the minority of gamblers who develop related problems. As Griffiths (2008) has noted, in an age of widespread internet access we are reaching the stage where the majority of people have a computer with potential access to an online casino in the home. It was estimated in 2006 that there were almost one million regular online gamblers in the UK, a third of the European total (Orford, 2011). Regulation of online gambling is difficult and of particular concern is the fact that young people, who may be more susceptible to developing gambling problems, can easily access online gambling environments, many of which offer little in the way of age verification checks (Orford, 2011). At the same time, some of the agencies which exist in the UK to provide help for the 300,000 people who have gambling-related problems in any year have developed an internet presence and the use of online environments for helping those who get into difficulties.

CASE STUDY

Gamcare

Gamcare, a UK-based charitable body, provides a telephone counselling service and also a parallel, online service called Netline. This is offered from 8 a.m. to midnight daily. A forum and a chat room are also provided. Notably, two-thirds of those using the online counselling services are under the age of 35 (Gamcare, 2010, p3). Those who use the internet most are unsurprisingly more likely also to use it to access help and support. Gamcare report that 47 per cent of those using their internet counselling service gambled on the internet compared with just 15 per cent of those who gamble elsewhere. As well as their own online services, agencies like Gamcare can signpost people to practical

Continued

CASE STUDY *continued*

online devices such as blocking software which prevents a user from accessing gambling websites. Typical feedback from users of these services includes comments to the effect that Netline is a lifesaver, invaluable *and a* Godsend *and the resources on the website have helped to turn many lives around (Gamcare, 2010, p9).*

Gamcare is at www.gamcare.org.uk and their telephone number is 0845 6000 133.

Playing computer games is one of the most popular leisure activities. Game technologies are often highly advanced and have recently been applied in therapeutic ways. For example, games based on solution-focused therapy have been used with adolescents with behavioural problems. The service user and the worker sit together and both interact with the game, named *Principal Investigator*. This approach has been found to help the development of therapeutic relationships and engagement with a service (Coyle et al., 2009).

The Samaritans have been training volunteers to listen to those in distress since 1953. In 1992 they also began to use email and then extended to the use of mobile technology and SMS (short message service) messaging to make their services more available in a digital age. Visit the Samaritans website at www.samaritans.org and explore some of the online help and support resources which are offered.

If you work in the mental health sphere there are an increasing number of examples of technologies being applied for therapeutic ends. With lengthy waiting lists to see practitioners of cognitive behavioural therapy (CBT) and evidence that manual and self-administered treatment can be effective, CBT is being offered via online computer-aided packages with good outcomes (National Institute for Clinical Excellence, 2006). The national guidance from NICE recommends some specific online packages including 'Beating the Blues' for people with mild to moderate depression and 'Fear Fighter' for people with panic and phobias. Details of these can be found at: www.beatingtheblues. co.uk and www.fearfighter.com. Such programmes are usually accessible following referral from a GP. We have here further examples of the possibility of reinforcing exclusion via the assumptions that are made by those who design and provide such digital resources. Many require certain levels of literacy and language skills and some feature videos without transcripts, which exclude those with some disabilities.

We have noted that a number of aspects of the welfare state are increasingly becoming digital. The above examples illustrate how specific therapeutic interventions are also being offered online. The example shows that such developments can offer certain unique advantages and, contrary to some expectations, anonymous online therapy can be just as effective as face-to-face therapy.

In an era in which welfare services are being scaled back there may well be occasions in which you struggle to find relevant local services for your services users, or ones which can be funded by the authority or agency for whom you work. As noted earlier, governments favour the development of online services which may reduce the costs of provision. Although the internet is often a solution, we should be aware that many people, and particularly those with whom social workers come into contact, remain digitally excluded and there is a danger of retrenchment into residual online welfare. In other words when welfare spending is being significantly scaled back and it is technically possible and less expensive to provide basic welfare services online, this may become the only avenue of access, as the choice of face-to-face encounters with local welfare providers is steadily removed.

The digital welfare state: Welfare benefits

The coalition government announced in 2010 one of the biggest reforms to the national system of welfare benefits since the founding of the welfare state. One of the cornerstones of a new system was to be universal credit, a new single payment to households which would be a major simplification of the previous system. In proposals for this new system the government made great play of the place of technology:

> *The department for work and pensions will be responsible for the delivery of universal credit and will make extensive use of online technology to allow people to better manage their claim and understand the benefits of entering paid work . . . Claims for universal credit will normally be made through the internet, and most subsequent contact between recipients and the delivery agency will also be conducted online.*

> (Department for Work and Pensions, 2010, p37)

Here we have another example of the scope of government ambition in relation to use of digital services and also the potential for major problems given that being in receipt of welfare benefits and being digitally excluded are categories that tend to go together. The system is due to be introduced in 2013. It remains unclear how the government will ensure that those who cannot access universal credit online will not receive a residual and poorer service. Social workers have always played a key role in ensuring that individuals and families access welfare benefits to which they are entitled. It will be important that they remain strong advocates for those who are socially and digitally excluded and who experience difficulties in accessing the new universal credit.

There is one other aspect of the new policy in relation to welfare benefits to which we would like to draw attention at this point. The coalition government were very adamant that they would reduce the significant amount spent on welfare benefits for those who had been judged unfit for work at some point. The aim was to reassess all of the two and a half million people in receipt of incapacity benefit and move those deemed fit for work according to a new points-based system onto a lower rate Jobseeker's Allowance. Once again technology has become central to the large-scale operation of these 'work capability assessments'. The information technology firm ATOS were brought in to conduct computerised assessments. The case of Larry Newman illustrates graphically potential flaws in the system. Larry had a degenerative lung condition that made it impossible for him to carry on his job, working in a wood veneer showroom. Despite Larry's difficulties in breathing and walking and having lost three stone in weight at this point, the work capability assessor awarded him zero from a possible 15 points and deemed him capable of work. Larry and his family appealed with the support of the Citizens Advice Bureau. While waiting for the appeal to be heard Larry died from his condition. A select committee report in July 2011 found evidence that assessors were over-reliant on standard tick boxes on computerised forms, and were not physically examining people or engaging them in eye contact or meaningful discussion of their situation (Work and Pensions Select Committee, 2011). The company responsible for the assessments has promised better staff training and improved standards. Again, it is clear there will be a significant role for advocacy for those who are incapacitated and subject to these assessments. Social workers, along with welfare rights campaigning groups, have a part to play in ensuring that assessments are completed fairly and that the use of technology is balanced with appropriate human interaction.

Procurement

Public sector spending by the UK government was more than £230 billion a year in 2010 purchasing goods, services, equipment, care services and construction; over a third of total public expenditure (Adetunji, 2011). One third of this took place at central government level, and a large amount at local government level. The cuts foisted on local government by the national coalition government in 2010/2011 led to an increased and sharpened focus on finding efficiencies.

You may wonder about the relevance of decisions about loo rolls and laptops to the important social work business of helping vulnerable people. However, if your local authority can pay £350 for a laptop, rather than the £2,000 paid by the neighbouring authority for the same computer, or £85 rather than £240 for the same printer cartridge (these are genuine examples from English councils), then it may well have a bigger budget for front-line social care work. The internet has played a key role in making procurement smarter and more efficient, in that it makes it quicker and more straightforward to compare the costs of similar items from a range of suppliers. There is an increasing tendency to open up and delegate decisions about certain aspects of procurement to those on the front line. There are parallels here with the development of the 'brokerage' role for social workers; a role which involves shopping around to find the best-quality and most appropriate services for the service users you are working for. So, whether it is finding supplies for your office or sourcing activities or personal assistants to support your service users, a key skill for the twenty-first-century social worker is to be able to compare information from a wide range of sources in order to find the best available within the resources available. Of course, this does not necessarily involve the internet but without it you will have access to far less information and choice. The national online procurement website at www.buyersguide.co.uk illustrates this well. If you look at this site you will see links to every local authority and you will also see the range of services and organisations that are listed.

ACTIVITY **2.3** *SOURCING INFORMATION*

Joe is partially sighted and paraplegic. He wants to have a new computer and to be able to access the internet. Where would you find information about hardware and software which is suitable for Joe? What aids and adaptations might be needed? If possible talk to other people with these impairments and ask them about their experiences, or talk to colleagues. Visit and search for suppliers at Buyers' Guide at www.buyersguide.co.uk, the RNIB at www.rnib.org.uk, Sight and Sound at www.sightandsound.co.uk and AbilityNet at www.abilitynet.org.uk. Which of these websites do you think is the most useful? What are the strengths and weaknesses of each?

COMMENT

On the Buyers' Guide website, under the heading 'Disabled Access,' you will find links to companies which supply assistive technology. This website is often used by local authorities. For the visually impaired, software which recognises speech and converts it to text, or screen text to audio or Braille output, is useful. The RNIB website is a good starting point for information on such products. For those with injuries and impairments which limit the use of limbs there are a number of hands-free alternatives to the use of a computer mouse. Sight and Sound or AbilityNet will have further information.

The third sector and digital access

Government policy in the UK for some years has been to involve the third or charity sector more heavily in the delivery of public services. The sector has been seen as having advantages over the statutory sector in terms of being more flexible, more trusted and tuned in to the needs of the local population and being able to deliver more for less cost. The sector may also have advantages in relation to getting people online and in delivering online services. As can be seen from a number of case studies, learning about computers and the internet works best when instruction is delivered by a trusted friend or local organisation (see the example of Digital Circles of Support in Chapter 5). For this reason, as noted by the Race Online 2012 campaign, *local charities are a fundamental part of trying to bring disadvantaged groups online because of their trusted relationships with those that they serve* (Lane Fox, 2010a, p47).

CASE STUDY

Signposting to better information

StartHere is a national social enterprise. They describe themselves as connecting people to vital support in times of transition, crisis or distress. They have developed an independent signposting service that provides users with a single point of access for information on a range of health and social issues. Through a simple-to-use interface, the service connects people to the most relevant services which might meet their needs and the database includes local and national, statutory and voluntary sector agencies. The service offers this example of Joe.

Continued

Joe left prison having served his sentence for drugs offences. Family relations had broken down, and with nowhere to go on his release, Joe found himself in the Ellison House Probation Hostel. There he had access to regular support, help with finding training for work, and access to drugs counselling. Joe was feeling more positive and getting ready to move on from the hostel when he heard that his father had died. Joe was subsumed by guilt and anger and unresolved emotions and the probation staff were worried that he would seek comfort in his old ways. His Senior Probation Officer had recently overseen the installation of the StartHere signposting service on a touch screen in the hostel and, looking at the section on bereavement, found the Waterloo Community Counselling Centre which offers bereavement counselling to local people. He commented: 'Residents here often will have no knowledge that there could be help locally for them. Since we have had StartHere available in the rest area I have seen a number of the residents looking for help finding jobs and housing advice. Staff actively encourage residents to use the touch screen to find answers for themselves, as they are sometimes reluctant to talk about really sensitive issues to people in here.'

(StartHere, 2009)

ACTIVITY **2.4** START HERE

You can explore the touch-screen application described in the example above. Go to the Start Here website at www.starthere.org.uk and find information about the touch-screen application. Follow the links. Use the map to explore services in your region of the UK in relation to the following: Coping and Caring; Crisis; Families; Housing; and Rights and Services.

COMMENT

Although the amount of content provided varies across regions, we suggest that the site provides clear and useful information. This will be a user-friendly resource to recommend to service users for a wide range of issues.

In relation to the theme of signposting, in an era when many health, social care and welfare services are being offered online as the default option, it is imperative that welfare professionals are familiar with the online landscape and can signpost service users to the most appropriate support. If service users do not have internet access at home it is important that you can put them in touch with local sources of access, such as libraries and community organisations. Signposting to sources of support and funding for provision of equipment and training to establish home access should also be considered. Access may also be denied or be limited for those with impairments. We have seen that although there is equalities legislation in place which should ensure access, many related policies have neglected this issue. In Chapter 3 we will elaborate on this theme.

CASE STUDY

Switched on communities

Earlier we asked you to visit the website of AbilityNet at www.abilitynet.org.uk in order to familiarise yourself with some of the range of assistive technologies which exist. This organisation furnishes another example of a third-sector organisation providing some of the most effective practical support to help people overcome the digital divide. Switched on Communities was a project run by AbilityNet with the support of DSGi (owners of PC World and Currys.digital). The project had four charity partner organisations: Age Concern (now Age UK); the Hope Foundation; Keyring; and Leicester Centre for Integrated Living. They also brought on board a range of partner organisations in eight different communities. The aim was to provide other community and voluntary organisations with resources and specialist expertise in training and resources so that they could support disabled people to access and use technology in order to bring within easy reach everyday tasks such as banking, shopping, communicating, education, volunteering and work opportunities. The programme provided organisations with the following:

- *training showing how to adapt computers to meet the needs of disabled users;*

- *resources which offered alternatives to using a keyboard and mouse;*

- *software to support struggling readers and CD-Roms with further information;*

- *help and support to identify the access needs of learners including the use of an online assessment tool.*

CASE STUDY

Get connected

Another example involving third-sector organisations is more directly related to social care. A partnership between the Social Care Institute for Excellence (SCIE) and the charity Technology Trust has led to the Get Connected Investment Project. This is a capital grant scheme for registered providers of adult social care in England and independent sector organisations supporting personalisation in adult social care. The aim is to improve access to technology for service users, carers, visitors and staff, and there is an emphasis on training and learning. By 2011 some 300 social care providers had received grants to invest in suitable technology.

System error

System Error was the title of a report from the Institute for Government on government information technology (IT) systems (Stephen et al., 2011). A task force of experts on IT, civil servants and business leaders assessed the history of government IT programmes and made recommendations for a new way of approaching the issue. They noted that despite some successes, such as online payment of vehicle road tax and automated payments of certain welfare benefits, there were many more expensive failures. Examples quoted include the National Offender Management system, NHS IT systems including Connecting for Health and the Rural Payments Agency system. They noted that despite spending up to 16 billion pounds a year, government IT always seemed very costly and suggested that government departments have not always procured the most up-to-date or appropriate technologies and systems that are available. This may be partly to do with lengthy procurement processes but could also be due to lack of appropriate information and choices at the time of procurement.

They recommended a new 'agile' or flexible approach which involves front-line staff more and allows more response to changes as systems and services develop. They also recommended that common standards such as those produced by the world wide web consortium should be used and promoted by government. It is important that IT systems which support and underlie public services are fit for purpose and can perform. When large-scale spending programmes by government in the public sector do not achieve the desired results it is often public sector workers who are left to deal with the resulting human problems.

Responding to this and adding a further note of caution the influential House of Commons Public Accounts Committee warned in 2011 that public services should not be made 'digital-by-default' until they are proven to work for their intended users including those without access to the internet at home (Public Accounts Committee, 2011).

Another example of the government assuming that the internet could provide a solution for a problem which is most acute for those who may well lack access came in the advice given to consumers in the face of soaring energy bills in late 2011. The Prime Minister and the Energy Minister urged consumers to shop around for the best tariffs, using all of the available evidence. Aside from the fact that many of the least well off have energy meters and a range of other barriers which may prevent them from accessing or being offered the best deals, it is very clear again that the poor, who are most likely to be digitally and socially excluded, are least likely to be able to use online comparison sites to find the best deals for energy prices. They will be reliant on advocates such as the Citizens Advice Bureau and Age UK at a time when those agencies are facing severe retrenchment and a lack of advisers to provide such guidance.

The examples presented and discussed in this chapter should give a sense of how many public and welfare services are available online (and sometimes available *only* online). Whether applying for welfare benefits, for social housing, or for health advice; whether looking for therapy, completing a tax return or finding the best product or service for the social work office, all of these processes can be facilitated and made more convenient using digital technologies, for those who can access them. The two caveats are that many people remain without straightforward access to the technologies and that the technologies are often more expensive and more problematic than forecast. We will elaborate much further on issues of digital inclusion and exclusion in Chapter 3.

We have tried to show both policy and practice. Further examples which are more directly related to student placements and to social work practice are assessed in Chapter 5. As you go on to placements and practice as a social worker, we hope that you will be attentive to how much digital exclusion is entwined with other forms of social exclusion and that you will use your social work skills and your knowledge of law, policy and other agencies to advocate that service users should be digitally included.

CHAPTER SUMMARY

- Government policy has been moving increasingly towards making digital methods the standard method of accessing all public services. This primarily means the internet, though other channels such as digital TV are also included.

- Shifting the way in which the public access services to largely digital channels may lead to large cost savings for the state. There can also be real benefits for service users in terms of quicker, more accessible and more responsive services, and more interactivity with service providers.

- A range of examples illustrate the development of both policy and practice in relation to digital provision of services. These include examples from housing, the NHS, welfare benefits, procurement and examples from the mixed economy that constitutes the provision of welfare in the UK (public, private and third-sector organisations).

- A significant minority of the population remain digitally excluded for a range of reasons. A number of national policies and strategies have been developed and implemented to tackle this digital exclusion, but as we move towards digital-by-default services it is not obvious that access by default will also be ensured.

- Several laws that social workers will be familiar with are relevant. Use of the law and knowledge of policy can help in advocating and empowering people towards digital access.

- The history of the adoption of large-scale technology programmes by government is replete with cautionary tales and expensive failures. Those who work in the public sector are often left to deal with the resulting human problems.

FURTHER READING

Lane Fox, M (2010a) Digital manifesto for a networked nation. Available at www.raceonline2012.org

This document provides a good deal of context and a lot of facts and figures to illustrate the patterns of digital inclusion and exclusion in the UK. It is optimistic in tone and emphasises the benefits to individuals and the nation of getting more people connected digitally.

Warren, M (2007) The digital vicious cycle: Links between social disadvantage and digital exclusion in rural areas. *Telecommunications Policy*, 31 (6–7), 374–88.

The focus is on rural areas but this paper analyses very incisively the ways in which digital and social exclusion can reinforce each other in a vicious circle. Warren particularly illustrates how, in spite of, or even because of, government policy which drives inclusion for the many, economies of scale mean that the smaller number who remain digitally excluded suffer even greater problems.

SCIE (2011) *Getting connected to e-learning: A short guide for social care providers.* Social Care Institute for Excellence. Available at www.scie.org.uk

The Getting Connected programme has enabled many care homes, domiciliary care agencies, and other providers of social care to adults in England to make much greater use of information technology, in order to improve the quality of life of their service users and also to improve the training of staff. This short guide gives a good overview of some of the ways that the delivery of social care is and can be shaped by the use of technology.

Chapter 3
Digital equalities and digital divides

. . . the prevailing view was that for the Minimum Income Standard to meet its criterion of allowing people 'to have opportunities and choices necessary in order to participate in society', working-age adults needed to be able to access the internet at home.

(Davies et al., 2010, p15)

A C H I E V I N G   A   S O C I A L   W O R K   D E G R E E

This chapter will help you to develop the following capabilities, to the appropriate level, from the Social Work Professional Capabilities Framework.

- **Professionalism.** Identify and behave as a professional social worker committed to professional development.
- **Values and ethics.** Apply social work ethical principles and values to guide professional practice.
- **Diversity.** Recognise diversity and apply anti-discriminatory and anti-oppressive principles in practice.
- **Justice.** Advance human rights and promote social justice and economic well-being.
- **Knowledge.** Apply knowledge of social sciences, law and social work practice theory.
- **Critical reflection and analysis.** Apply critical reflection and analysis to inform and provide a rationale for professional decision-making.
- **Contexts and organisations.** Engage with, inform, and adapt to changing contexts that shape practice.

See Appendix 1 for the Professional Capabilities Framework diagram.

The chapter will also introduce you to the following academic standards as set out in the 2008 Social Work Subject Benchmarks:
5.7 Work effectively with others.
5.9 ICT and numerical skills.

Introduction

Chapter 1 introduced the impact of a digital society on its citizens. This included ideas around the social shaping of technology whereby internet use mirrors existing patterns of social exclusion and marginalisation. In Chapter 2 we looked at the digitisation of social policy and implications for the social work profession. In this chapter we will look more closely at the parameters of digital access for service users. We will begin with assistive technologies and the ethics of digital interventions for supporting independent living via Telecare and Telehealth, before moving on to the digital divides relating to internet access. You may already have seen how differential digital access affects participation in a digital society. As social workers you could find yourselves dealing with the complexity of digital divides which involve multiple parameters of access. In these cases, your knowledge about the diversity of ways in which people need support to use computers and access online environments could make a significant difference to establishing and maintaining independence. Over five centuries ago the British philosopher Francis Bacon stated that *knowledge is power* and when it comes to supporting digital inclusion this phrase is worth remembering. All too often there are solutions to enabling digital access but they involve overcoming a range of barriers and this chapter will help develop your own knowledge about exclusion with useful directions for further information and advice. The theoretical position used throughout this book is that of the social model of disability (Oliver, 1981) and this chapter begins with the development of this model and the challenges posed to traditional medical views of impairment and illness. We will be revisiting the theoretical concept of the social shaping of technology and examining the social and cultural significance of access parameters. These underpinning theories offer useful frameworks for considering the dual potential of technology for both enabling and denying inclusive digital practices.

The social model of disability

Social equality and social justice are core foundations of social work and it is likely you will have chosen the profession because you care about equality of access to resources and welfare services. In the twenty-first century, social work education and practice subscribe to a social barriers model whereby inequalities of opportunity are related to the failure of society to recognise and cater for diversity. Prior to this, physical impairment or other medical conditions were viewed as the primary sites of disablement and the individual concerned was seen as someone tragic to be pitied rather than as a social and cultural opportunity for changing the environment to enable and support participation. These older charity and medical models of disability have created mixed implications. On the one hand they offered an explanation for symptoms and a potential gateway to treatment, support and welfare benefits, but on the other they led to the negative stereotyping of impairment with a particular focus on the discourse of tragedy. This had negative consequences for those deemed to be handicapped or crippled by their own bodies and the social model challenged such negative attributions. Developing out of the identity politics and equality movements of the late twentieth century, the social model of disability was a radical vision which claimed that the built environment and contemporary cultural discourse were discriminatory and disabling forces (UPIAS, 1976; Oliver, 1981). Not everyone accepted the social model and there were claims that it failed to take into account individual pain and physical limitations (Shakespeare, 2006) but the call for greater acceptance of difference and diversity did create radical changes to social practices. Alterations in language have resulted in words like handicap and cripple no longer being socially acceptable and concepts like inclusive practice are built into organisational policies and procedures. An early example of inclusive practice in the built environment was the provision of ramps in public buildings. Originally designed to enable wheelchair access, they are now also appreciated by people pushing prams or buggies or who have shopping trolleys or suitcases on wheels. Although there is rarely a one-size-fits-all solution to access, ramps have helped promote increased understanding of how changes for some can create an improved experience for everyone.

The social nature of external barriers to access of resources brings important considerations for social work practitioners and it will be useful to keep the principles of the social model of disability in mind as you read through this chapter. Consider the position and strength of the social model today, several decades on from the time it first emerged. When you next look around the external built environment, it is likely you will see a resurgence of obstructions on pedestrian walkways such as flower containers, public art or water features with no indication of their presence. You may live in a town where shared surfaces have been introduced. These remove the distinction between the pavement and the road. Such changes suggest that physical barriers to access to the built environment are returning to urban areas and the focus on inclusive environments is becoming diluted. Keep this in mind while reading through this chapter; and note in particular the nature of the multiple barriers faced by service users in relation to their access to digital technologies and the internet.

Assistive technology

The enabling potential of assistive digital technology can be exciting but unfortunately the reality does not always live up to the promise. Local authorities have a legal obligation to provide aids and adaptations and as social workers you may find yourselves involved in initial assessments or making referrals to occupational health teams and other health and social care staff for the provision of independent living aids. It is important to be aware of the potential access implications of all digital assistive technologies; in particular where there is disparity between the expectations of devices and the actual experience of using them.

The primary role of assistive technology is support for independent living. Dominant health issues in an older population include dementia, the risk of falls and a range of chronic health conditions. Increasing life expectancy has led to increased demands on welfare services. Different systems detect, predict and intervene in different circumstances and offer vital support for remaining independent in the community or within the home. The benefits of assistive technologies are not limited to older people but can provide support for all ages, in particular individuals with sensory, physical or cognitive impairments. Advanced electronic devices offer choice and control over many day-to-day tasks which are problematic and enable communication and access to information via digital channels in ways which would not otherwise be possible. Research carried out by the Papworth Trust into disability suggests that 17 per cent of people are born with impairment and the remaining 83 per cent acquire one in later life (Papworth Trust, 2010). In these cases, digital technologies can play an important role in supporting the performance of tasks which would otherwise be difficult as well as ensuring the safety with which these tasks are carried out. In addition to this, technology is increasingly being seen as a means of reducing the cost of hospital and residential care as well as providing cost-effective and independent maintenance of personal health and well-being.

There is growing interest in the affordances of the internet for provision of a range of digital support services. You may already know about cases where the internet has been used to provide access to information about individual medical conditions or welfare benefits or to develop self-help groups and provide access to counselling and other therapeutic services. For many people who live alone or in isolated rural areas, the internet can be a valuable source of communication, retail opportunities and entertainment and we will be looking at the assistive technology which supports computer use and internet access, in particular for service users with physical, sensory or cognitive impairments, later in this chapter. First, we will look at assistive digital technologies in the home and ethical concerns which have been raised around their use within domestic and community environments.

Assistive technologies in the home

Assistive technologies support individuals to do things they are no longer able to do unaided. For example, a memory jogger can be used as a reminder to take medication, a liquid level indicator to minimise spills and a speaking clock or watch for telling the time. There is a large range of assistive technology and not all of it is digital in nature, for example a walking stick, a mobility cane or a clothes grabber, but all assistive technology shares the aim of supporting independent living. Digital assistive technology can be high tech or low tech, relatively simple to operate or more complex in design. The Social Care Institute for Excellence (SCIE) in their *Research Briefing 28: Assistive technology and older people* suggest three categories of technology grouped according to their role (Beech and Roberts, 2008, p2).

- *Supportive technologies* These help individuals perform tasks they may be finding difficult. Examples include video entry systems and medication reminder units.

- *Detection and reaction (responsive) technologies* These help individuals manage risks and raise alarms. Examples include gas, fire and water detectors and panic buttons.

- *Prediction and intervention (preventative) technologies* These help individuals to prevent dangerous situations or to raise alarms. Examples include fall predictors, movement sensors and monitors for assessing vital physiological signs.

These three categories offer a useful insight into the variety of assistive technologies which are available to support safety and provide potential assistance in ensuring independence and reducing social isolation. The SCIE report stresses the importance of ensuring that intervention through assistive technology is achieved sensitively and with agreement between the service user and provider on its relevance and role, in particular when it is part of a care package under the personalisation agenda. Digital assistance is commonly part of a package of support known as telecare which aims to manage risk and focus on individual safety. Research is ongoing into the use of more complex, personal digital devices which monitor vital signs and feed this information remotely to health care professionals. This developing area of intervention is known as telehealth.

RESEARCH SUMMARY

Assistive technology, ethics and dementia

The SCIE Report 30, Ethical issues in the use of telecare *(Perry et al., 2010), summarises areas to be considered when supporting people with cognitive impairment to use assistive technologies. Researchers adopted an ethical framework with these four principles.*

Autonomy: the ability of an individual to make choices *Autonomy is related to independence and choice in everyday life, which is often taken for granted. Reliance on professional or family carers for safety monitoring can drastically promote or restrict autonomy.*

Beneficence: the principle of working for the benefit of the individual *Telecare has the potential to benefit people. It can provide assurance and confidence and reduce unwanted dependence on professional staff or family carers. It can also increase personal comfort through environmental sensors and controls.*

Non-maleficence: the principle of doing no harm *While telecare can benefit an individual, it also has the potential to expose people to risk. A balance must be achieved between ensuring safety and invading privacy. The potentially stigmatising effect of telecare should be recognised and minimised.*

Justice: the moral obligation to act on a fair adjudication between conflicting claims *In the interests of justice, resources for telecare services should be allocated so as to balance the needs of the individual with those of the wider community.*

To find out more about the use of assistive technologies and dementia visit the SCIE website at www.scie.org.uk. Here you will find free dementia video resources and the SCIE e-learning resource 'The Open Dementia Programme'. You may also find it useful to view the programme called 'Telecare: The Ethical Debate' which can be found on SCIE's Social Care TV at www.scie.org.uk/socialcaretv

CASE STUDY

Family resistance

Stan lost his eyesight five years ago. He has a computer with screen-reading software and has learned to touch type; he now wants to have the internet at home. Stan is proficient in using his screen-reading program but is getting bored with word processing. His wife Mary is interested in genealogy and when they visit their son and his family 15 miles away, Mary uses the internet to research her family tree. Whenever Stan mentions that he would like his son's help to set up the internet, his son refuses to take him seriously. He tells Stan it would be better for him not to go online because he might end up doing something stupid like selling the house by accident. Stan has worked out that they can afford the monthly payments but he wants to go online with his son's blessing and not for it to cause an argument. Being online might keep Stan occupied and entertained and improve his quality of life. Alternatively he might get into difficulties as his son predicts.

Telecare

A digital society is one with increasing reliance on technologies for communication and information to support individuals living alone and service users with mobility or medical conditions. The term telecare is used to describe the provision of remote emergency support via a telephone landline. A typical telecare system consists of a digital unit with a microphone and speaker. An alarm is raised either through an individual pressing an alarm button or from a set of sensors around the house. Sensors can detect changes in the physical environment such as a flood, gas, smoke and heat. Alarms are triggered if there are unexpected movement patterns such as a sudden fall or an untypical lack of movement. The personal alarm button is designed to be worn all the time so the alarm service can be contacted wherever the person is located in the home. Some alternative types of alarm consist of pull cords which are situated in high-risk areas like bathrooms. Once the alarm has been triggered it can be directed to either a control monitoring centre or to a carer's mobile telephone. The call handler or carer then speaks to the person and assesses the situation in order to decide whether further intervention is required. There are stand-alone control boxes which can enable a carer within the same house to monitor potential or actual alarms without control centre involvement. The control box receives signals from sensors which are positioned in a variety of different places depending on their purpose, for example on a bed or an exit door. These set off a vibrating pager to alert the partner or carer within the home that their attention is required.

Telehealth

The term telehealth describes equipment which is used to monitor the vital signs of people who have long-term illnesses such as chronic obstructive pulmonary disease (COPD) or diabetes. Telehealth is being piloted in several areas in the UK in order to collect evidence of its cost-effectiveness. The evidence base for remote management of people with long-term chronic illness is currently being developed. However, in financially stressed times with increasing demand on available services, it is highly likely that investment in the piloting and evaluation of systems to create remote links between individuals and doctors will continue. Telehealth monitoring equipment can collect and collate medical information such as pulse rate, temperature or blood pressure. This has the potential to reduce the necessity of visits to hospitals and clinics for regular tests as well as support individuals in the self-management of their conditions and health. In the not too distant future, we may well be seeing increased telehealth provision of health and social care in the day-to-day management of chronic and long-term illness.

A digital society supports innovative practice. Developments are continually being made which sequentially progress the affordances of new and existing technologies. The telehealth industry is an example of this. We can see how the pull cords, button alarms and sensors used within telecare are being extended to digital devices which give more personal information about their user. At the present time these new health monitors still require the individual to interact with them, but the technology already exists for fabrics and other skin-contact devices like pads that use mobile and wireless frequencies for transmitting data. Cardiac devices such as pacemakers, defibrillators and insulin pumps already use active embedded or implanted components and have the potential to provide monitoring information automatically. It is likely that health and social care services will be adopting more remote monitoring systems in the future.

As well as individual devices, research is ongoing into the use of existing devices in the home such as television, computers and smart phones to support health and well-being. You may already be familiar with the use of webcams and internet services such as Skype which can provide digital face-to-face contact, or have experience of instant and text messaging being used to provide educational content. Online digital calendars which send out reminders of important dates can be adapted to provide prompts for medication or other interventions. Much of the research on the use of internet technologies for health care has been carried out in other countries, in particular the USA. If you are interested in finding out more about the potential of digital health services there is plenty of information available online. However, always keep in mind the potential experience of the service user who may not have the background and experience necessary to feel confident with digital technologies.

ACTIVITY 3.1 *TELEHEALTH: POTENTIAL ADVANTAGES AND DISADVANTAGES*

Telecare is offered routinely but full evaluations of the effectiveness of user-controlled, digital telehealth systems are still being developed. To find out more visit the King's Fund website at www.kingsfund.co.uk. Search for telecare and telehealth within the website. You will find a large number of resources including a number of evaluations of the benefits of these systems.

What do you think are the potential advantages and disadvantages? Take five minutes to write down some notes and compare them with the comments below.

COMMENT

You may have thought of some or all of the following potential advantages and disadvantages of telehealth systems.

Advantages

- *Increased flexibility and choice.*
- *Empowers and offers greater personal control.*
- *Early interventions save longer-term damage to health.*
- *Supports independent living.*
- *Reduces hospital and residential care admission.*
- *Frees budgets which can be used for other social services.*

Disadvantages

- *No substitute for face-to-face care.*
- *Devices may be unusable for some.*
- *Creates isolation not empowerment.*
- *Chance of misunderstanding or misreading leading to unnecessary worry.*
- *Insufficient service-user involvement in the development of digital health care technologies.*

Ethics of assistive technology

The use of remote monitoring systems in the home is often promoted as a valuable contribution for maintaining health, mobility, well-being and security. But they can just as easily be seen as posing potential threats to individual privacy and autonomy. For example, at which point does monitoring someone's night-time behaviour move from care to control? As social work students you will be familiar with the role of values and ethics in social work. While developments in the use of technology for care can offer benefits they also raise ethical concerns, in particular with regard to those considered vulnerable or frail.

Ethics in social work is a complex area. It involves examination of our own values in both our personal and professional lives, as well as identifying the impact of external influences. During your course you will be introduced to the idea of potential dilemmas created by conflict between personal values and those expected of you as social work professionals. You will learn about non-discriminatory practice and gain an appreciation of diversity and the politics of difference. You will be familiar with the multiple discourses of discrimination such as ableism, ageism, racism and sexism which inform many examples of oppressive practice and know that core to the social work agenda is the adoption of anti-oppressive ways of working in order to promote equality of opportunity within an inherently unequal society. The ethics with regard to using assistive technology can incorporate some or all of these considerations.

When considering the ethics of care, it is useful to bear in mind that assistive technologies should not be assumed to be the only solution. There may be other non-technical forms of assistance which could be more appropriate. Rather than a device which monitors falls, it might be possible to reduce potential trip hazards in the environment. Instead of a sensor which detects an overflowing sink or bath, an automatic overflow detector which releases a plug could offer a less invasive solution. Where decisions regarding the use of assistive technology need to be made, they should always be taken in consultation with the people concerned. Different people react in different ways and something which is supportive for one person might well be a source of confusion for another. If the person has dementia this raises further ethical issues around informed consent and data protection.

The SCIE Adult Services Report 30, *Ethical issues in the use of telecare*, summarises the ethical issues involved in supporting people to use telecare services. These are primarily concerned with ensuring the technology used to monitor people's movements and activities does not threaten their choice and privacy. The report highlights the need for appropriate assessment and informed consent along with correct data protection procedures applied to any personal information which is collected. The report stresses the potentially isolating effect of assistive technologies when used as part of a telecare package and the importance of not considering them as an alternative to direct social care or informal support unless, of course, this is the expressed wish of the person using the service and they have full mental capacity (Perry et al., 2010). The report highlights the tensions between policy and practice and the need to balance potential conflict between meeting policy aspirations and dealing with the realities of front-line practice. The research informing the report focuses mainly on the use of telecare to support adults with a cognitive impairment, including dementia. These groups are likely to be the most vulnerable so good practice here will be applicable to all service users. Similarly the ethical principles defined within the report can be equally well applied across all developing technological care solutions.

In Chapter 1 and at the beginning of this chapter we referred to the social shaping of technology. Assistive technology should never be seen as neutral or inherently beneficial. Its use must be carefully examined to ensure that it will provide maximum benefit to the service user and that there is no non-technical alternative which might be worth consideration. Assistive technology is often rejected by people who may deny any potential benefits on the grounds that it would make them feel stigmatised. In the same way that many visually impaired people refuse to use mobility canes in the belief that they are visible indications of vulnerability, so service users may decline offers of wearable alarms, telecare units or fall monitors on the basis of personal pride or fear of being labelled with a disability. At the beginning of this chapter we looked at the social model of disability which sees individuals as disabled by their environment rather than by personal medical conditions or impairments. The social model has highlighted disabling barriers in the environment and assistive technology which reduces environmental obstacles can be seen as an example of the social barriers model in practice. However, the medical model of disability, which positioned disablement in the body rather than in external surroundings, remains influential and the words 'disability' or 'disabled' continue to carry negative connotations, in particular for older people. To be labelled disabled in the past often carried a sense of tragedy, as well as derogatory implications, making it something to be avoided at all costs. Refusal to consider technological assistance for independent living should always be taken seriously as deep-rooted worries and fears could be underlying individual resistance.

Assistive technology: Access enabled or access denied

Technology is not always the most appropriate answer for everyone but the right technology for the right person can make a significant difference to supporting independent living and safety in the home, in particular where correct ethical procedures and the appropriate communication channels have all been adhered to. Unfortunately, when it comes to assistive technology there is no one-size-fits-all model. The processes of manufacture rarely include research into exact requirements with regard to usability or accessible design. Research has conventionally been informed by a traditional, individualist medical model of disability, which focuses on a solution to a problem in the individual rather than a social one which calls for attention to attitudes and the built environment. Calls for changes in the social relations of research production have led to the promotion of participatory and emancipatory research paradigms. These place greater relevance on the lived experience of individual service users and have potential to become part of the solution to removing barriers to access rather than further imposing them (Oliver, 1992). However, research into exclusive design practices is not extensive. The greater part has been based on case studies and is largely observational (Beech and Roberts, 2008). Where research is funded into the application of assistive technology, it has found discrepancies between the fields of design and engineering and the requirements of the recipients. This disparity has only recently been challenged by calls for universal design and the construction of technologies which are accessible by all. The frustration for people working within social care can be in seeing how the potential for inclusion is being lost through exclusive design practices. If greater attention were paid to the needs of the users of assistive technologies, and to supporting the customisation and personalisation of devices to individual requirements, then usage could be significantly enhanced. Instead, many technologists remain fixed within the paradigm of a medical model which views the technology as a fix, or an external sticking plaster approach. Assumptions are made about access and usability, which are rarely based on the experience of the service user, and these influence the design and manufacture process. Unless companies take note of the voices of service users then exclusive design practices will continue.

ACTIVITY 3.2 DIGITAL BARRIERS

Experiences with digital technology can be positive and involve a real sense of achievement at mastering the working of a complex device. But for many people the reality is more negative. Encountering a device for the first time, without the necessary prerequisite knowledge, can be a daunting experience. Think about a new digital device such as a mobile phone or a digital television which was unfamiliar to you. How did you set about learning to use it? Make some notes about your experience and see how many potential barriers to access you can identify.

COMMENT

Your list of barriers might include some or all of the following:

- *Manuals only available online or on a CD-ROM.*
- *Instructions are too complex.*
- *Premium rate telephone helpline.*
- *Online-only help.*
- *Unable to locate appropriate tools.*
- *Buttons too small.*
- *Fear of breaking power connector.*
- *Too many functions.*
- *Not understanding the purpose of the function.*
- *Over-complex menu systems.*
- *Lack of interoperability between old and new devices.*
- *Incompatible software or file formats.*
- *Feelings of inadequacy and failure.*
- *Negative emotions, such as impatience, frustration, anger and despair.*

The internet and digital divides

Home access to the internet was a defining feature of the first decade of the twenty-first century. At the start of the year 2000, many homes were establishing connections through dial-up modems which in turn were replaced by faster broadband services; wireless access has now become the default for many organisations, the education sector and the domestic consumer. Chapter 1 has already looked at the revolutionary effect of digital information and communication on society and its potential for enabling a digital democracy will be examined next.

CASE STUDY

The benefits of online communication

Joyce has three grandchildren. When her son's marriage broke down, her daughter-in-law moved away leaving Joyce with less contact with the children. By using email Joyce has managed to keep in touch throughout their adolescence. Joyce took a class in computer basics at her local community centre which covered how to get online and set up an email account. It included attaching and downloading files so that Joyce could send and receive digital photographs. The IT manager gave Joyce advice on buying a computer and a volunteer helped to set up her up with a home internet connection. The grandchildren are now grown up and two of them are living abroad. By learning to use Skype, Joyce can do more than send emails. Skype software enables free phone calls to be made over the internet. By using a webcam, Joyce is able to turn these phone calls into video calls so that she can talk to her grandchildren as well as see them online in their new homes. A year ago, Joyce's husband died, leaving her living alone and feeling isolated. Her computer has helped her feel less lonely as she has her emails, not just from her grandchildren but also from people she has met on holiday, which she can read and reply to. Joyce doesn't use the internet for browsing. She finds websites difficult to navigate and doesn't trust the internet for shopping but she does enjoy the benefits of digital communication with family and friends.

There is a major difference between print and digital data which is often unrealised. The printed page can be magnified but the content still remains fixed as printed text. Once converted to digital text, however, there is greater potential for customisation to suit individual preference. Text can be enlarged, the font changed and colours and contrasts altered. As well as adjusting the appearance, and magnifying the screen, there is technology for enabling speech to be converted to text and text into speech. You may already have experienced alternative ways of using a computer other than the standard keyboard and mouse. If not you might want to visit a website like AbilityNet at www.abilitynet.org.uk. AbilityNet is a national charity which helps disabled adults and children use computers and the internet by adapting and adjusting their technology, making it easier to use. There is a vast range of alternative input and output devices available which offer the potential for computer use to anyone regardless of physical, sensory or cognitive impairment. You might also try WebAim at www.webaim.org. This is a US site focusing on accessible digital access and it offers an introduction to web accessibility which contains information and videos about assistive technologies and the diversity of ways people use computers and go online.

RESEARCH SUMMARY

The invisibility of digital exclusion

The government is moving to digital-by-default delivery of services and the construction of a digital welfare state, in spite of research which suggests that the potential for digital exclusion aligns with existing categories of social exclusion. While government initiatives focus on provision of mainstream access they fail to address digital exclusion for users of assistive technologies, in particular the inaccessible nature of the internet itself which assumes that people are mouse users and can see the screen. Government reports refer to 8.5 million people who have yet to get online, but focus on the four groups below. This data was taken from Building the networked nation, the last leap to get the UK online (Race Online, 2011b).

Young and excluded *Age 15–34 with an income of less than £10,000, barriers include lack of a fixed address. This category includes young parents, young singles, singles with poor employment prospects, singles with low incomes or dependent on benefits.*

Uncertain and unpersuaded *Age 55 plus with an income of £10–20,000 plus, barriers include lack of motivation, skill, knowledge and an element of cost.*

Traditionalists *Age 65 plus with an income of £13–30,000 plus, barriers include mistrust of technology, lack of motivation, skill, knowledge.*

Sheltered seniors *Age 75 plus with an income of £7–10,000, likely to be widowed and living in sheltered accommodation, barriers include little exposure to new ideas, declining capabilities and cost.*

How do you interpret this exclusion of users of assistive technologies, who face additional barriers of cost, training and support and exclusive digital practices? What does this suggest about current government attitudes towards the social model of disability which calls for society to identify and challenge external barriers to access and participation?

CASE STUDY

The inaccessible internet

Diana has limited peripheral vision and uses a screen reader to access the internet. Screen readers read website text out loud but because they read out everything, including navigation instructions, they can be difficult to use, in particular if the websites have not been designed with the needs of screen-reading technology in mind. Diana likes cookery programmes on the television and wants to look up the recipes using the internet address which is given at the end. Diana knows that if she keys in the internet address on the browser page it will open the website. She has carefully copied down

Continued

the address and typed it in. Unfortunately the website has not been designed for screen-reading technology and her program starts to read out all the unnecessary background information and the links which surround the main text. There is no Skip to Content command and although Diana knows how to jump through the headings using her keyboard, she cannot find the recipe she wants. After several frustrating attempts, and getting lost with numerous links and instructions which she doesn't understand, Diana gets upset with herself and switches the computer off. Well-crafted websites support users who want to access content by listening rather than seeing. If all websites were designed in this way then a significant number of barriers to access would be reduced.

Barriers to digital access

Whether digital technology is an aid for independent living or for supporting access to the internet, the key barriers are similar. However, this section will address the use of computers and internet access. There are three layers of barriers, starting with cost, followed by the provision of appropriate training and support, and finally the inaccessible design of digital content which fails to adapt to individual access requirements. We will examine each of these in more detail because unless you have personal experience of working with someone requiring assistive technologies to go online, you may not be aware of the additional and significant layers of barriers which have to be overcome.

Cost

Unless you have bought assistive technology, the high prices may surprise you. While the cost of mainstream computer technologies has decreased over the past decade, the cost of assistive hardware and software has failed to come down. If anything, the gap between the two has increased. As is the case with aids for independent living, assistive computer technology is a niche market. This makes personal shopping problematic and means there is less competition in terms of price. While standard laptops, keyboards and mice can be found in supermarkets and mail-order catalogues, roller balls or joystick mice, large-size keyboards and other alternative input and output devices such as pads and switches remain the provenance of specialist suppliers. Optimistic advertisements for these products can be misleading, in particular with regard to software programs like text-to-speech and speech-to-text which necessitate a steep learning curve. Expert assessment and a trial opportunity is always a valid recommendation. For students and employees there has been central funding available to buy necessary equipment through the Disabled Student Allowance (DSA) and Access to Work schemes, although these grants are continually being reduced. Some charities offer bursaries or other small funds to support the digital inclusion of those not in education or employment at a local level, but the demand generally outstrips the supply. The cost of computers and internet access remains very much down to individuals to manage and for those operating outside a narrow range of access criteria, and who are on fixed incomes, the high prices can contribute significantly to their digital exclusion.

Appropriate training and support

After the barrier of cost there is a second layer which centres on individual confidence and competence in operating within digital environments. For some people this may involve poor literacy skills, or it may be unfamiliarity with using a standard keyboard and mouse which prevents them engaging with new digital ways of working. In some cases it can be the alternative assistive technology itself, which family and friends are unfamiliar with and unable to use. The need for appropriate training and support in developing the necessary confidence and competence with new ways of working should not be underestimated. It may be worthwhile remembering how you felt when faced with a new software program or an unfamiliar mobile phone and you were unsure of where to begin. One option is to look at the manual or help information but this is frequently provided in an online-only version which assumes an internet connection and the ability to see the screen and navigate effectively through the pages. If you need technical support during your studies there is usually a computer help desk you can turn to or technical support available through your employer. Advice from family and friends might also be sought.

For users of assistive technology, finding the appropriate support can be more problematic. Standard help desks are rarely equipped to deal with queries outside of the mainstream operating systems or software packages and where help is advertised as being available through specialist suppliers this often uses premium-rate phone numbers. While experts in specialist technology may have the skills to troubleshoot problems, it is difficult to appreciate the uniqueness of individual situations. Technical support for assistive software is a specialist area. It requires expert knowledge of the hardware and software as well as awareness of the different permutations which can occur with a variety of different users. It is highly unlikely that individual problems will present themselves in similar ways so distance telephone or online support requires high levels of patience, experience and interpersonal communication skills. Assistive software programs, in particular text-to-speech or speech-to-text, require extensive periods of time to adopt to new ways of working. While some packages offer training, either as part of the overall cost or as an added extra, this is frequently given at the beginning with additional support at an extra cost. Users of assistive technology who have mobility restrictions may be unable to attend a local college or community class and find they are restricted to using their computers in isolation at home where the barriers to access can be invisible. Family and friends who are also unfamiliar with these new ways of working may experience equal frustration. The result is often that expensive equipment is put back in the box and back in the cupboard.

CASE STUDY

Digital exclusion

George needs to register for housing assistance but the local housing association (HA) only accepts online applications. The resource centre George attends has one computer in the manager's office and this is rarely available. The HA say if George makes an appointment at their main office someone will help him fill in the forms but when he turned up he didn't have all the necessary paperwork so had to leave without making the

Continued

---

application. George has tried to access the internet at his local library but didn't have the necessary proof of residency required to open an account and use the computers. There is a community centre on the High Street which has a public access computer but there is always a queue. George isn't experienced with a keyboard so is nervous about using a computer. A friend has told him the online application cannot be saved and returned to later but has to be filled in all at once and is time limited. George doesn't know if this is true but the thought puts him under pressure and makes him even more apprehensive.

Exclusive design and delivery of resources on the internet

We have looked at two layers of barriers to access to digital ways of working; the cost of assistive technology and the need for appropriate training and support. The third layer is most commonly encountered where the first two criteria have been met. When the assistive technology has been purchased, and the training and support are in place, if the digital materials and resources have not been designed with the needs of the technology in mind then individual access will continue to be denied.

International accessibility guidelines for digital content were laid down by the Web Accessibility Initiative (WAI). This was formed in the 1990s in the early days of the internet and the world wide web. Unfortunately, not all web designers pay attention to the WAI guidelines. This has resulted in a proliferation of inaccessible content, designed and delivered on the back of assumptions of very narrow ranges of access criteria. These assumptions can be usefully described as the MEE-Model of computer access. MEE stands for Mouse, Eyes and Ears and describes the way the majority of people operate in digital environments, in particular web designers and ICT technicians and specialists. They use a mouse to navigate around the screen, their eyes to see content on the monitor and their ears to listen to audio resources, prompts and announcements. The problem with following the MEE-Model is that it then becomes easy to assume other people are using their computers and accessing the internet in the same way. The model fails to take into account the multiple alternative ways of operating within digital environments using computer adaptations and assistive technologies. It is narrow assumptions of access criteria like these which lie at the heart of digital exclusion.

The inaccessible nature of content on the internet is not a new phenomenon. In the late 1990s, when the internet and the world wide web were first made available for public use, the potential for digital democracy was seen as a primary function.

Worldwide, there are more than 750 million people with disabilities. As we move towards a highly connected world it is critical that the web be usable by anyone regardless of individual capabilities and disabilities. The W3C is committed to removing accessibility barriers for all people with disabilities – including the deaf, blind, physically challenged, and cognitive or visually impaired. We plan to work aggressively with government, industry, and community leaders to establish and attain Web accessibility goals.

(Berners-Lee, 1997)

The importance of ensuring digital democracy was a key driver. In the same year, the move towards internet equality was evident.

> *The users in our project are the Web users with a disability, like visually or hearing impaired people. The needs for these users are to access the information online on the internet just as everyone else. The impact of this project on the users with disabilities is to give them the same access to information as users without a disability. In addition, if we succeed making web accessibility the norm rather than the exception, this will benefit not only the disability community but the entire population.*

(Dardailler, 1997)

We need to be asking ourselves why users of assistive technology continue to be increasingly disabled through exclusive digital practices, in particular the design and delivery of resources and services via the internet. The barriers we have looked at are structural in origin so you may already be making the connection with the social model of disability because there are no technical reasons for digital exclusion. If you think of high-profile users of assistive technology such as the physicist Stephen Hawking or the late film actor Christopher Reeve, you will see that there are few limits to the physical adaptation of computers to support people experiencing severe restrictions of speech and movement. However, for the majority of individuals already disabled by society, digital disablement represents an additional layer of exclusion; one which has potential repercussions for access to health and social care services in an increasingly digital-by-default society.

ACTIVITY 3.3 WHY SHOULD I GO ONLINE WHEN I DON'T WANT TO?

There are multiple reasons for digital exclusion and you are likely to encounter a range of different attitudes towards the internet. Think about your family, friends and other people you know through the different spheres of your life. Have they all been online? Are there any notable exceptions? Not everyone wants to take part in the digital revolution which is sweeping across our society. Take a few minutes to consider some of the reasons people might give for not having an internet connection, for not wanting to adopt a digital lifestyle or for refusing to access services online.

COMMENT

You may have thought of some or all of the following reasons for resistance to digital ways of working.

- *Lack of interest.*
- *Preferring face-to-face encounters.*
- *Physical, sensory or cognitive impairment.*
- *Computer prices.*
- *Cost of internet connection.*

Continued

COMMENT continued

- *Lack of confidence.*

- *Unable to use a computer.*

- *Too much information on the internet.*

- *Library has closed down.*

- *Too old to learn new things.*

- *No one to help.*

- *Lack of computer classes.*

- *Benefits the government more than individuals.*

- *Language barriers.*

- *Restrictive cultural practices.*

- *Poor or non-existence internet connection.*

CASE STUDY

Digital exclusion for younger people

Joe and Magya have three children and live in a two-bedroom flat on a large urban estate where their only income is state benefits. They have a computer donated by Joe's sister but it is several years old and the software is out of date. They cannot afford a telephone landline and have no internet access. Katy, the eldest child, goes to school where she is often set homework which involves using the internet. Katy finds that even if she saves the work she does in the school library onto a data stick supplied by the school, she can't open it at home because she doesn't have the necessary programs. Sometimes she tries to do her essays at home but the keyboard has several keys which stick and there is no ink in the printer. Compatibility problems make it difficult for Katy to transfer her work between the home and school environments. To use a computer at the local internet cafe costs money and her friends don't have internet access either. Her best friend Helen doesn't even have a computer at home.

New technologies have been described as a double-edged sword; one that is related to social stratifications and can either reduce divisions in society or amplify them (Warschauer et al., 2004). We've become familiar with the notion of digital divides as complex and dynamic phenomena (Van Dijk and Hacker, 2003). We have seen how cost, lack of support and exclusive digital environments are barriers for those with ambitions for digital engagement, but there are other multifaceted dimensions which involve attitudes to technology and the perceptions around its usefulness in individual lives. Selwyn suggests it is a lack of meaningful use, rather than technological or even psychological factors, which determines engagement with ICT; *the reality of their use is based around a complex mixture of social, psychological, economic and, above all, pragmatic reasons.* (Selwyn, 2004, p349).

The government is setting up a digital welfare state based on digital-by-default access to information and services. Digital exclusion is recognised but solutions are primarily located in a supply of mainstream access through cheap off-the-shelf laptops which assume a narrow range of access criteria, or community centres which fail to cater for complex personalisation needs of individuals using assistive technology. In the meantime, platforms for discussion and debate in the public sphere are also moving to digital-only participation and this is creating a double exclusion for those on the wrong side of the digital divide.

> *An emergent risk is that differential access to familiarity with technology can reinforce social inequalities and add to the vulnerabilities of individual and social groups that are most in need of social work intervention.*

(Steyaert and Gould, 2009, p742)

As we come to the end of this chapter, you should have gained a better understanding of how digital divides are not simply about access to new technologies but involve broader and more complex issues around the cost, support and quality of that access. It is worth reconsidering the connection between social work and digital exclusion.

> *This is where the concept of the 'digital divide' becomes pivotal: the risk of less access to services as well as less choice and possibly greater costs may result in social exclusion because the person does not have access to new technology or skills to use that technology. This is also where social work becomes involved, as one of the professions fighting social exclusion.*

(Steyaert and Gould, 2009, p743)

To be digitally excluded is to be increasingly marginalised from mainstream ways of working, with the danger that digital disability is becoming a new twenty-first-century category of social exclusion. For social workers, whose daily practices involve support for vulnerable sections of society, already disadvantaged and disempowered, instances of digital exclusion are likely to become more relevant to daily workloads, in particular as essential welfare services, vital to the day-to-day lives of service users, continue to move to digital-by-default provision.

CHAPTER SUMMARY

- Research shows that the potential for digital exclusion is following existing patterns of social exclusion, thereby adding an additional layer of disadvantage onto those already experiencing marginalisation and disempowerment and increasing the complexity of digital divides.

- There are significant gaps between those designing and developing assistive technology and those using it in day-to-day life. This has resulted in digital devices not fulfilling their potential and users becoming disadvantaged in a digital society rather than supported and empowered by its affordances.

Continued

CHAPTER SUMMARY *continued*

- The social model of disability calls for greater acceptance of diversity and difference and places disablement in the external structures of the built environment and cultural attitudes. Digital ways of working which follow a narrow range of access criteria rather than recognising the diversity of ways in which people operate are creating new categories of digital disability.

- Government moves to digital-by-default provision of information and services has potential implications for social work with its value base encompassing equality of access to resources and opportunities, resulting in the consequences of digital exclusion appearing in caseloads and assessments.

FURTHER READING

Age UK (2009) *Introducing another world: Older people and digital inclusion*. Available at www.ageuk.org.uk

A useful guide to digital inclusion and exclusion for older people including insights into personal attitudes to digital technology and internet access.

CEG (2009) *Consumer Expert Group report into the use of the internet by disabled people: Barriers and solutions*. Available at www.webarchive.nationalarchives.gov.uk

Now archived and in danger of being forgotten, this is one of the best guides produced to date on the use of the internet by people already disabled by society who are now facing digital exclusion. The report highlights barriers to access with useful suggestions for removing them.

Oliver, M and Sapey, B (1983; 2006) *Social work with disabled people: British Association of Social Workers (BASW) Practical Social Work*. London: Palgrave.

This book is a classic text for all social work students working with disabled people. It offers an analysis of disability from the perspective of the social model and the revised edition promotes the view that if social work is to empower then the social model of disability must be adopted as a theoretical foundation.

Perry, J, Beyer, S, Francis, J and Holmes, P (2010) *SCIE Report 30: Ethical issues in the use of telecare*. SCIE. Available at www.scie.org.uk

An important summary of the ethics of using technology to support independent living. There is guidance about steps to follow pre-installation and post-installation and the importance of ensuring the protection of the rights of the individual.

Steyaert, J and Gould, N (2009) Social work and the changing face of the digital divide. *British Journal of Social Work*, 39 (4), 740–53.

This article covers the historical development of the term digital divide and the research into the parameters of digital access. It introduces an aspect not covered in this chapter, which is the choices around content preference found in different socio-economic groups.

Chapter 4
Digital tools for virtual learning

Honours graduates in social work should be able to use ICT methods and techniques to support their learning and their practice.

(QAA, 2008)

Introduction

When you first came to university to study for your social work degree, you may not have expected information and communication technologies (ICT) to be relevant to your course. Social work is about people and it is likely to have been the social aspect which called you, rather than any desire to work with computers or develop your digital literacies. However, as we have seen in both Chapter 1 and Chapter 2, the internet has become integral to all professional environments and social work is no exception. On placement and in practice you will be expected to operate efficiently within a variety of digital environments and while you are studying you will find lots of opportunities to develop the prerequisite digital confidence necessary for professional practice. Apart from developing digital competencies, there are other reasons for addressing the social impact of new digital ways of working and in Chapter 3 we took a closer look at the relationship between digital exclusion and social exclusion and at how those already experiencing social disadvantage are likely to become digitally excluded as well. As a social work practitioner you will often find yourself seeing both sides of the digital divide between those with access to the internet and those for whom that access is problematic or even denied.

During the past decade, social work education has had to continually adapt to ensure that students are equipped with the appropriate digital literacies and able to think critically about the impact of social shifts to digital ways of working. This chapter will examine more closely the relationship between digital information and communication technologies and the social work degree. It will begin by showing how these technologies have always been part of the curriculum and how this requirement has evolved to keep up with wider social change. This is followed by a section on the concept of graduate attributes and transferable skills. In this section we will be making particular reference to the use of the internet for communication and the management of information. Next we will take a broader look at the delivery of teaching and learning content in digital formats. This includes virtual learning environments, e-portfolios and a range of Web 2.0-style digital tools and social media. Finally, we will consider the cognitive effects of the internet and look at the research which suggests digital ways of working are changing the ways in which the brain processes and analyses information. By the end of this chapter, you will have a clearer understanding of how your social work degree not only prepares you for entry into a challenging and rewarding profession, but also ensures that you are equipped to operate effectively within the digital environments you will find there. You will see how your own critical engagement with digital ways of working can support and develop awareness of the social impact of digital exclusion, especially for the service users whom you may soon be meeting in your social work placements and practice.

ICT and the social work degree

Underpinning your learning modules are programme benchmarks issued by the Quality Assurance Agency (QAA) in partnership with the General Social Care Council (GSCC). These benchmarks are the standards against which your degree is measured. They define what is expected from you in terms of understanding of your subject. In 2004, the GSCC required all social work degree courses to include an assessment of the computer literacy of their graduates. Initially, this requirement could be met by the European Computer Driving Licence (ECDL) or an equivalent qualification. The ECDL was a competency-based accreditation which assessed individual skill levels in the following seven areas:

- word processing
- spreadsheets
- database
- presentation software
- email
- file management
- internet browsing

At a time when computer literacy was the new badge of professional practice, the ECDL was considered an appropriate measure of ICT competency. At the start of the twenty-first century, the social work profession was undergoing a paradigm shift from analogue to digital ways of working and ICT skills were increasingly vital. However, the requirement for social work graduates to have the ECDL or equivalent qualification was changed in 2008 when the QAA Social Work Subject Benchmarks were revised and the criteria attached to graduate ICT competencies expanded. The aim was to ensure that social work education was keeping up with changing times, in particular with regard to the social impact of an increasingly digital society. Subject Benchmark 5.9, ICT and Numerical Skills, reflected the criteria seen as appropriate for social work practice in a digital age. It described how social work graduates should be able to use digital methods and techniques to support their learning and their practice and listed the specific areas where information and communication technologies were considered to be particularly relevant and necessary. The full details of the subject benchmark can be seen in Appendix 1.

It is clear from looking at the benchmarks that the ECDL skills are still necessary but there is additional focus on the application of those skills to practice. For example, using ICT effectively for professional communication, data storage and retrieval and information searching still requires confidence and competence with word processing, email, spreadsheets and database, but with additional knowledge about appropriate communication and safe and secure management of data. The benchmark criteria support specific higher education competencies of independent learning and critical thinking, in particular the processes of 'reflection on practice' which lie at the heart of the social work experience. Attention to the ways in which ICT can be used to support, develop and enhance these processes creates valuable opportunities to develop digital competencies. The most significant amendment to the revised subject benchmarks was critical awareness of the social impact of the internet and of digital divides. This major change, less than a decade from the development of the first social work degree, is indicative of the speed with which digital ways of working were being adopted and the move to online delivery of information and services. The ECDL had focused on computer literacy but failed to address the social implications of exclusion from digital ways of working.

At the time of writing changes relating to social work students and their ICT competencies were being discussed. In 2011 the Social Work Reform Board (SWRB) agreed a set of recommendations for selecting the best candidates onto the social work degree. They produced a set of admission guidelines which included the recommendation that applicants must possess the appropriate information technology skills prior to the start of their programme and demonstrate a basic ability to use IT effectively. A minimum requirement would be for programmes to be sure that applicants could use email, the internet, word processing tools and have an understanding of the issues of data storage and protection prior to being offered a place. The guidelines are further evidence of the potential implications an increasingly digital society is having on the social work profession (Holmstrom, 2011).

You may already have been familiar with computers and the internet before you started your social work degree, but not considered the wider impact of a digital society or felt it was particularly relevant to social work education. Alternatively the idea of acquiring digital literacies may have felt daunting and not really what you expected when you started your course. This chapter has been written to help you gain a better understanding of how your social work degree offers opportunities to increase your own digital competencies in a safe and secure environment.

Transferable digital skills

One of the key advantages of a higher education experience is the adoption of extra-curricular proficiencies called graduate attributes. These are based on the concept of transferable skills; those additional qualities you pick up indirectly, sometimes without even realising you are learning because the processes are more practical than academic. Transferable skills include: effective interpersonal communication, time management, organising your own workload, teamwork such as being able to settle disagreements, and leadership qualities such as showing initiative in problematic situations. Purposely engaging with digital technologies as part of your learning process will help you to adopt a number of transferable skills which will be useful within placement and future employment. If you are a social work student who is feeling uncertain about using computers and the internet, this section of the chapter might be particularly reassuring. Whether we like it or not, it is no longer possible to ignore the impact of technology on higher education or professional practice so it will be useful to take advantage of digital ways of working during your studies where you are in a safe and supportive environment. This section looks at three areas where the internet has become integral to learning: digital communication, digital information resources and digital teaching and learning materials environments. By examining these in turn, you will see how studying for your social work degree helps increase your transferable skills with digital ways of working.

Digital communication

The use of email has become ubiquitous, often becoming a substitute for letters and partially replacing telephone calls. At university email is the primary means of communication between staff and students. Even if you were not a regular email user before you started your course, you can expect people to contact you this way and expect you to check your email for new messages on a regular basis. Alongside emails, there are associated digital calendars which can be shared with colleagues. These have facilities for inviting people to meetings or checking other people's availability. They can be set to send you reminders of things to do and places to be. An electronic email-linked diary is a valuable organisational tool. You will also need to become familiar with the online management of your timetable. In particular make a note of bank holidays when libraries or printing facilities may be closed or operating on reduced hours, for announcements of network down times when you will be unable to access virtual resources and for important deadlines such as assignment submission dates.

ACTIVITY *4.1* *EMAIL ADDRESSES*

At university you will be given an email address linked to your student account. Students often redirect their university mail towards their personal one. What does your personal email address say about you? Have you tried to create a unique identity or used a complex combination of punctuation or spelling? Did you favour a name which was slightly risqué rather than bland? Your choice of email address may be more important than you realise. What do you think when you see email addresses like these:

- *hotsexytoys@gmail.com*

- *dumbdizzybimbo@yahoo.co.uk*

- *spannerallan@gmail.com*

- *3y8Xella19SW@talktalk.com*

COMMENT

What might have seemed like an amusing email address for communicating with family and friends may be less appropriate for presenting a mature, professional image, especially when applying for part-time work while you are studying or communicating with the person assessing your suitability to be a professional social worker. By all means continue to use your personal address for family and friends but have an additional one for professional purposes. This should be non-controversial, politically correct and, if possible, easy to remember with a minimum of numbers and punctuation marks.

Some universities will use text messages to communicate cancelled lectures or other last-minute changes. Mobile phones with internet access make it possible to keep in continuous touch with other people through email, text and social networking sites like Facebook and Twitter. Many universities have official Facebook and Twitter sites and there is more information about these later in this chapter. There are specific issues around the use of social networking sites, in particular Facebook, within professional employment and in particular within social work placement and practice, and these are addressed in more detail in Chapter 5.

Digital systems are used for the majority of university administrative procedures. You may have already experienced the UCAS online admissions process. During your time at university you will be expected to access administrative forms and procedures including timetables and examination dates online. These will be available through an institutional network or an intranet like a portal and it will be worth taking the time to understand these navigation systems and search facilities. There are many different information storage systems available and each one can feel as if it is presenting you with a new learning curve, but the more you persevere, the more your confidence with operating within new digital environments will increase.

Digital information resources

The university library is becoming an increasingly digital place. As well as enabling you to borrowing physical books from the shelves, your library will offer you virtual access to a range of digital information sources including e-journal databases and ebooks. If an e-learning environment is new to you it can seem confusing at first, especially when different e-publishers use different platforms, making it difficult to find consistency of navigation or style. However, it really is worth taking time to become familiar with these different environments so that you see their variety as offering opportunities for acquiring digital confidence. There will always be staff on hand to help if you get into difficulties and most libraries run training workshops on digital searching and referencing.

You may find the processes involved in borrowing physical resources are also becoming computerised. In many libraries a bar code scanning system has been installed to allow borrowers to take out and return books. Your electronic library catalogue will be accessible both on and off campus. Here you can check the availability of books as well as reserve them and renew them online. The library catalogue will include ebooks as well as physical ones; these often include the more popular titles, which means increased availability of key titles on your set reading list. Reading books online is different from having the printed copy in front of you but there are advantages to their any time any place availability and if you have not used them before, it is worth trying them out. Ebook reading platforms are becoming increasingly sophisticated; many now allow you to make digital notes while you are reading and some will allow a small proportion of pages to be printed. The availability of portable readers such as the Kindle and the iPad is also adding to the popularity of ebooks. There are sites on the internet where you can download ebooks; many of these are classic titles which are out of copyright and now available at no cost.

RESEARCH SUMMARY

Project Gutenberg

Project Gutenberg digitises books which are out of copyright restrictions. It makes them freely available on the internet for people to read online or download onto mobile e-book readers. The project is named after the Gutenberg Press which was invented in the late fifteenth century and made possible the mass distribution of printed materials for the first time. Project Gutenberg aims to do this with digital text. Its philosophy is to make books available to the public in formats which the vast majority of the computers, programs and people can easily read, use, quote and search. There are three components to the Gutenberg Library: 'light' literature such as Alice in Wonderland, Peter Pan *and* Aesop's Fables; *'heavy' literature such as the Bible, the works of Shakespeare and 'Paradise Lost'; and reference materials such as* Roget's Thesaurus *and sets of encyclopedias and dictionaries. As well as access to digitised books, Project Gutenberg has opened up the process of digitisation. Apply to become a Gutenberg volunteer and you are given digitised pages to proofread and check for errors. Another part of the project is to invite volunteers to burn CDs and DVDs for people without internet access so that they can take advantage of this fantastic free literary resource. For more information about the project and the books which are available to download free visit www.gutenberg.org.*

As well as ebooks, your university library will contain collections of e-journals stored in a number of different e-journal databases such as EBSCO, LexisNexis and JSTOR. These databases store thousands of digitised journals which can be searched by author, title, subject or keywords. If you are not familiar with journal databases you might find the Applied Social Sciences Index and Abstracts (ASSIA) a useful place to begin. ASSIA provides references and summaries of articles covering social services, social work, sociology, education and health. Another collection you may find useful is Social Services Abstracts. This offers abstracts of articles for over 1,300 journals in areas including social work, welfare and mental health services. Journals are valuable sources of peer-reviewed academic research which will support you in the writing of your assignments. The majority are copyright protected which means your library pays a licence fee each year and you will need a password to access them. While on campus you might not realise these are password-protected environments but when you try to access off campus you will find you are asked for an ATHENS password. This is an access and identity management service which provides an authenticated single sign-on facility. If you are not sure how to use it, check with staff in the library for help as the ATHENS system will ensure you can always access e-journal content if your institution has the appropriate licence. Newspaper databases will also be available through your library. These can be useful for social work students to examine how the media have reported high-profile social welfare cases in the past. If you are unable to find a particular journal article, book or other reference source which you need, there are inter-library loan facilities where items can be ordered from other libraries. The internet has not only opened up access to digitised content, but also made it possible for you to access the majority of the information resources you might need at the time and place of your choice. Taking the time to become familiar with the different sources of electronic information will help you make the most of all the resources which are available and develop confidence in searching and navigating through digital information environments.

As well as the wealth of institutional content accessible through your library, digital sources of information include the mass of content freely available on the internet. Unlike your university library, these resources need to be approached with caution. In Chapter 1 we examined how the free and open nature of the internet means there are no restrictions on content and anyone with access can upload materials. As students, you need to develop the appropriate digital literacies in order to separate peer-reviewed and academically credited knowledge from personal and unreferenced opinion. Effective use of search engines, in particular those which specialise in returning academic content such as Google Scholar at www.scholar.google.com, is a good place to begin. Learning to use appropriate keywords and phrases will help to return a selection of matching content although using the internet in this way may only return the abstracts of journal articles. Access to the full text version is likely to be restricted by copyright licence and, as mentioned in the previous section, you will need to use your university ATHENS account to gain access. Always be cautious when researching online and use recommended procedures for filtering and authenticating the validity of content.

One way to access good-quality digital content is to use the resource collections which have been developed by reputable organisations. These collections are often called repositories and consist of databases of links accessed through a single portal. An example is the Social Care Institute for Excellence (SCIE) at www.scie.org.uk. The SCIE website contains lots of materials which have particular relevance to social work education and their multimedia formats can add breadth and depth to your studies as well as offer a welcome alternative to text-based content. Becoming familiar with navigating around online resources such as these will help build confidence in accessing and exploring a range of different digital environments.

ACTIVITY *4.2* *FREE EDUCATIONAL RESOURCES ON THE INTERNET*

Visit the SCIE website at www.scie.org.uk to see examples of free, high-quality resources which will support your social work learning. These include modular multimedia courses on Personalisation, Communication Skills and Social Exclusion. SCIE's Social Care TV area offers both training resources and general interest programmes on topics relevant to current social care practice including Safeguarding Adults and Safeguarding Children. Also look at SCIE's Social Care Online which is a searchable database grouped into relevant topics including Government and Social Policy, Health and Health Care and Social Work and Social Workers.

COMMENT

Quality online resources such as those distributed by SCIE offer valuable learning experiences but learning online cannot replicate the experience of meeting other people. As online delivery is seen as a way of cutting costs and increasing efficiency, so face-to-face services are being reduced. For many service users this can mean increased physical isolation. The more you consider the consequences of digital practices while studying for your social work degree, the better prepared you will be when you qualify as a social worker in a digital society.

In this section on transferable skills, we have looked at ways in which digital communication and information management is embedded within social work education. The expectation that you will engage with digital ways of working at university may seem challenging at first. We have tried to reassure you that opportunities to engage with digital technologies will increase your confidence with digital ways of working. They will support the competencies outlined in the subject benchmarks and ensure that you are a digitally literate student and practitioner. In the next section we are going to look more specifically at how the processes of teaching and learning have taken advantage of the internet and some of the Web 2.0-style digital tools you might use during your studies.

Digital teaching and learning resources

Although face-to-face contact is still valued by both staff and students, the any time, anywhere convenience of online learning can enhance traditional lecture and seminar modes of delivery. The term Web 2.0 is often heard in relation to online learning and refers to the development of programs which support user-generated content. Web 2.0 means you can get involved. The first websites on the internet offered few opportunities for user interaction. In contrast, Web 2.0 websites are characterised by text-editing boxes. These mini word processing facilities enable users to key in content and upload it to the internet. There is no need for knowledge of programming as the software does all the conversion and Web 2.0 has made potential digital contributors out of everyone with the prerequisite means of internet access. Because of the collaborative nature of this software, it is often collectively referred to as social media and programs such as blogs and wikis have been adopted for use within higher education. In this next section we will look at some of the common digital tools you are likely to find.

Virtual learning environments: Digital tools for enhancing face-to-face delivery

All universities have some form of virtual learning environment, sometimes referred to as a VLE, for supporting face-to-face teaching and learning. Virtual learning environments offer flexible access to teaching and learning materials and using them is like having the resources of the university available to you off campus. They are particularly useful for students studying part-time or at a distance and offer valuable support for students who miss lectures due to illness or who have additional employment or care commitments and might not be on campus as much as they would like. Two common virtual learning environments are Blackboard and Moodle. Staff will use these for uploading a range of learning resources such as module guides, reading lists and lecture notes. Some staff may develop collaborative online activities within discussion forums, or set up blog or wiki facilities and encourage you to engage in online conversation and debate. If you are unfamiliar with the terms blog and wiki, you will find information on these later in this section. Institutional practice varies but virtual environments are often used for the electronic submission of assignments and to manage electronic marking. Some universities manage the whole assignment submission process online with marks and feedback available through an electronic grade centre linked to individual student accounts. Virtual learning environments have customisable home pages with a range of optional modules which students can arrange to suit their own requirements. As with all the other digital information systems you will encounter at university, try to welcome these as opportunities for useful engagement with different digital ways of working and a means of enhancing your digital capabilities and skills.

e-portfolios: Digital tools for practice placement

Critical thinking and reflective practice are integral components of higher education but they have a particular importance for social work students. During your course you will need to build a portfolio which demonstrates evidence of your critical reflection, of both your learning processes and your placement experiences. An e-portfolio will help you gather this evidence electronically, make it easier to move it around from place to place and to share some or all of this with colleagues, staff and assessors. It supports the use of multimedia content such as images, video, audio and web links and is useful for demonstrating a range of transferable digital skills such as communication and information management. The term e-portfolio refers to the end result as well as the tool used to create it. You may find an e-portfolio linked to your institutional virtual learning environment, such as the Blackboard e-Portfolio tool, or it might be a separate program like PebblePad or Mahara. Alternatively your university may have developed its own e-portfolio software. You may find you can choose to present your portfolio either as a collection of pages in an A4 folder or in an electronic version. If you have the choice between the two ways of working, it is worth considering managing the process electronically. If the thought of e-portfolio software feels like another learning curve in an already busy learning environment, then consider using word processing, presentation or desktop publishing software to produce and compile your content. This will still support the development of your digital literacies including electronic file management and organisation as well as helping you to develop additional confidence and competency with a range of digital formatting and editing tools.

Blogs: Digital tools for reflection

The name blog derives from the term weblog. These were lists of websites created by journalists in the early days of the internet as a means of quickly sharing information. Today a weblog or a blog is treated more like a diary. Content, called a post, is uploaded to the internet where it can be read by anyone or by a selected audience. Blogs have comment facilities for readers to post their own responses and this makes blogs a useful method of communicating and sharing ideas with like-minded people. Within higher education, blogs are often used as digital tools for reflection. While you are on placement, a practice log will be essential, but recording your learning experience for re-evaluation and reflection at a later date is also a valuable exercise. Reflective practice is integral to the deeper levels of learning and understanding you will be expected to demonstrate at university. It is also an example of a transferable skill which will benefit you in your professional career. Virtual learning environments such as Blackboard have their own integrated blog tools and blogging software is freely available on the internet. Blogger at www.blogger.com and WordPress at www.wordpress.org are two reputable programs. They include templates for you to personalise the appearance of your blog and they support the uploading and management of images and multimedia files. Many social work and social care organisations have their own blogs and these can be useful places to visit. Try the Social Work Blog on the *Community Care* website at www.communitycare.co.uk and the SCIE blog at www.scie.org.uk.

Wikis: Digital tools for collaborative learning

Wikis are similar to blogs in that they support user-generated content through posts and comments. However, wikis have an additional feature whereby readers can edit the original text and create a collaborative document. An example of this is Wikipedia, an online encyclopedia which is continually being edited and updated by its readers. Wikis are useful for encouraging online communication between groups of students, in particular for task-based activities such as sharing individual experiences or compiling anthologies of information. Virtual learning environments such as Blackboard have their own integrated wiki tools and wiki software is freely available on the internet. PB Works at www.pbworks.com and Wikispaces at www.wikispaces.com are two reputable programs.

RESEARCH SUMMARY

When the online encyclopedia Wikipedia at www.en.wikipedia.org was first constructed, many university lecturers condemned it as an unreliable source of knowledge. The processes whereby new knowledge was constructed and validated were traditionally lengthy and rigorous ones with dissemination managed by research institutions and large publishing companies. Wikipedia challenged this monopoly by enabling anyone anywhere in the world to access and contribute to an encyclopedia of knowledge. The idea that unknown individuals with no formal training or accreditation could write valid articles for an encyclopedia was quickly discredited by academics and in its early days, Wikipedia was not considered a suitable reference point for students. In 2005 Wikipedia challenged its critics and in a research experiment managed by the journal Nature, *reviewers took articles from Wikipedia and from the* Encyclopaedia Britannica *and compared them for accuracy (Giles, 2005). To the surprise of many people, the difference was less than expected. There were 2.9 errors per article for* Encyclopaedia Britannica *versus 3.9 errors per article in Wikipedia. The key difference was that the articles in Wikipedia could be corrected within minutes. Today, anyone submitting content for Wikipedia has to provide appropriate citations and reference sources. Moderators examine content for relevant source materials and if these are considered inadequate the article is labelled as being in need of further verification. Wikipedia articles often appear near the top of search results. If you are using Wikipedia always make sure the content is appropriately referenced within the article and check the references are all valid.*

Social bookmarking: Digital tools for managing information

Collecting and sharing lists of website addresses lay at the heart of the weblog which was the precursor of the blog. Today such lists of websites are often referred to as Favourites and the process of selecting them is known as bookmarking. When faced with the mass of information on the internet, it is important to have some way of managing those sites you know you will want to return to at a later date. As we have seen by looking at blogs and wikis, a feature of Web 2.0 software is the 'social' aspect; these programs are designed to be shared with other people. Delicious at www.delicious.com is an example of a social bookmarking tool which works in a similar way. Within Delicious you can select a website address and then categorise it with a number of personally selected keywords known as 'Tags'. Tagging is a typical feature of Web 2.0 software and is commonly used to collect and share information. You may have already noticed lists of tags underneath blog posts or on photo sharing programs like Flickr at www.flickr.com. Delicious uses tags as identification tools and automatically searches and collates other content which shares the same tag. You can share your own collection of websites and link with other Delicious users who have agreed to make their collections public. Within Delicious, tagged websites can be organised into groups which have similar themes; for example, 'older people', 'children and young families' or 'mental health'. Delicious can help you to manage large amounts of digital information quickly and efficiently. This can be particularly useful if you are carrying out research in preparation for an assignment or group project or want a more organised way of browsing the internet. Social bookmarking is a powerful method of sharing other people's searching experiences and can often lead to links to useful websites you might not otherwise have encountered.

RSS feeds and feed readers

RSS stands for Really Simple Syndication; it is a way to save time and be informed when new information is uploaded to your favourite sites on the internet. This is done by setting up a feed and accessing updates through a feed reader where different information can be organised into different categories. RSS feeds were initially used for keeping up to date with the news but can now be set up to track new content on social media sites like Facebook, blogs and wikis. Having an RSS feed to your favourite sites saves you from visiting them to check for new material. If a site has the RSS facility it will have a square orange RSS feed icon. Clicking this will display a list of the most recently added content to the site as well as different options to subscribe to the feed. In order to have easy access to lots of different RSS feeds, you will need to decide how you want to access them. You can do this via your browser settings, or some feeds support email alerts; there is also dedicated feed reading software which enables you to set up a separate site containing all your feeds in a single place. Examples of RSS feed readers are Netvibes at www.netvibes. com, Bloglines at www.bloglines.com and Google Reader at www.google.com/reader. To find out more about RSS feeds and readers go to Commoncraft videos at www.common-craft.com and search for RSS.

RESEARCH SUMMARY

Twitter and freedom of speech

An injunction has traditionally been used to protect identities in legal cases, in particular if lives were considered to be at risk, for example child offenders or serial killers. These injunctions have been referred to as gagging orders. At the end of the twentieth century, the European Convention on Human Rights was written into UK law by the Human Rights Act of 1998 and cases began to appear where the Act was used to extend the power of human rights to cover the right to privacy. This has been a controversial move, with some journalists and newspapers claiming the use of these superinjunctions was harming investigative reporting and that they were increasingly being used by powerful individuals and corporations for silencing the media.

The open and free nature of the internet supports freedom of speech and lies outside the jurisdiction of the courts. As social media sites such as the micro-blogging site Twitter have become increasingly popular so the instant transfer of information across the world has enabled people who might otherwise be silenced to have a voice and for that voice to be heard and passed on to others. Twitter has become the subject of controversy when users have ignored superinjunctions. Where newspapers and television have been prevented from revealing identities, names have been revealed through Tweeting. The online battles over freedom of speech have yet to be resolved. Software owners claim they are not responsible for the acts of individuals who post on their sites and, as many of these individuals register under pseudonyms, the courts are at the present time unable to impose penalties.

Social networking: Digital tools for communication

Social networking is the name given to sites like Facebook at www.facebook.com which support social communication. Many sites have their own media identities, for example YouTube at www.youtube.com is designed for sharing videos, Flickr at www.flickr.com for sharing images, LinkedIn at www.linkedin.com for professional networking and Twitter at www.twitter.com for short, succinct status updates of 140 characters or fewer. While Web 2.0-style tools such as blogs, wikis and social bookmarking have been welcomed as potentially useful tools for teaching and learning, the use of social networking sites has received a more mixed reception. Research has shown that students report uncertainty as to how these programs could best be used for educational purposes, preferring to maintain them for private communication networks between family and friends (JISC, 2008). Sites like Facebook have been particularly controversial within social work practice. In Chapter 1 we looked at some of the issues which have been raised about the blurring of boundaries between private and public behaviours, and the potential conflict between personal online identities and our professional working ones. These are important issues which need to be addressed. You do not want to make the mistake of posting private opinions about your colleagues or caseloads which then inadvertently become public knowledge. Your social work education involves preparing and supporting you for practice placement where you will find that there are particular requirements with regard to your use of the internet. Chapter 5 covers this in more detail.

ACTIVITY **4.3** *3D VIRTUAL WORLD SCENARIOS*

There are several advantages to participating in 3D virtual world scenarios. The simulation of real-life events in safe environments offers unique opportunities to practise in real-world situations. However, programs like Second Life are at the high end of the educational technology spectrum. Unless users are familiar with keyboard communication and on-screen navigation, 3D worlds can be challenging places. The multitasking involved in finding your way around, accessing resources and communicating with others demands a set of skills which can be discouraging rather than inviting. What other barriers can you think of to learning in this way?

COMMENT

Identified barriers might include:

- *High level of technical requirements needed.*

- *Good-quality graphics card needed.*

- *High bandwidth internet connection essential.*

- *New learning curves required in order to operate effectively within 3D digital worlds.*

- *Chat function requires familiarity and experience with this style of communication.*

- *Anonymity of personalised avatars might be alienating, in particular to users who prefer to know who they are talking to.*

- *Inaccessible for visually impaired users.*

Virtual worlds for teaching and learning

Learning through simulation is not new and problem-based scenarios designed to repli-cate real-life situations and offer opportunities to practise in safe environments were supported by early digital technologies. Multimedia CD-ROMs and web-based scenarios used combinations of video and audio to create realistic case studies but there was little opportunity for interaction. A more advanced opportunity for online problem-based learn-ing is the virtual 3D world of *Second Life* where education technologists are continually pushing the boundaries in the creation of digital learning spaces. *Second Life* has the potential for students to collaborate virtually through their avatars which are customisable digital representations of themselves. Through their avatars they can participate in semi-nars, attend lectures and explore alternative 3D environments which include real-world video and audio resources. These simulated environments give students opportunities to be involved in tasks and activities in a safe and controlled environment and experience situations which would not otherwise be possible.

The PREVIEW project created eight problem-based learning scenarios for paramedic students at St George's University of London and for health and social care students at Coventry University. The scenarios for the paramedics were designed to explore typical emergency situations with students having opportunities to ask the patient questions and carry out various observations and assessments. Students are given an equipment box containing resources they would routinely have available to them in real life and can select appropriate instruments and medication. The health and social care scenarios are set in a care home called The Cedars. There is an introduction to each scenario and students are given background information about their role and the problematic situation they are dealing with. To see examples from these scenarios go to YouTube at www.youtube.com and search for 'PREVIEW overview' which is uploaded by Learning Innovation. There is more information about the use of 3D virtual worlds in Chapter 5.

RESEARCH SUMMARY

Digital narratives

Digital narratives can serve multiple purposes within social work education and practice. In the past, traditional research methods frequently involved unequal power relations between the researcher and the research participants, particularly in investigations into the social effects of physical, sensory or cognitive impairment. Oliver (1992) called for a change in the social relations of research production, saying that disability researchers should not only investigate the parameters of existing oppression, but ensure that new knowledge and understanding were produced through processes of co-production with research participants. Research should be carried out 'with' participants and not 'on' them. Such participatory and emancipatory research methods align well with the values and ethics of social work education and practice, and digital narratives offer a powerful method for collecting and sharing the voices of service users who have histori-cally been silenced. Creating digital stories from photographs, audio and video not only enables research participants to have active involvement, it is a powerful learning tool for students. Digital case studies demonstrate the reality of a social experience and offer a

Continued

RESEARCH SUMMARY continued

deeper understanding of an alternative lifestyle or culture through the use of visual and audio media. Producing a digital narrative involves the processes of critical thinking and reflection which are integral to higher education and social work practice. The producer has to manage the skills of selection, rejection, sequencing and synthesising as well as the experiences of presenting with subsequent peer assessment. By their nature, digital narratives involve engagement with a range of multimedia formats. This enhances confidence and competence with working in digital environments and increases transferable digital literacies. For examples of the use of digital narratives visit the Stroke Stories website at www.strokestories.scot.nhs.uk.

Cognitive effects of digital engagement

So far in this chapter we have looked at some of the practical implications of digital ways of working on your social work degree. These have included adapting to digital systems and practices, the development of transferable digital skills and the impact of Web 2.0 tools on your learning experiences. In the final section of this chapter we will move away from the pragmatic use of the internet for teaching and learning and examine some of the broader cognitive effects of studying in a digital age. We will begin with the issue of plagiarism before looking at contemporary research suggesting that the shift to digital ways of working is changing the ways in which the brain manages and interprets information. We will examine the potential implications of these findings for learning and for the processes of critical reflective practice which are integral to social work education and practice.

Digital plagiarism

The word 'plagiarism' derives from the Latin plagiarius meaning an abductor or kidnapper. At university, plagiarism is commonly agreed to mean the wrongful taking of another person's work and passing it off as your own. This can be work copied from a book or the internet or from another student. In higher education, where the focus is on originality and evidence of the student's ability to demonstrate a unique understanding of their subject, plagiarism can have serious consequences, including failing an assignment or even a course. Plagiarism is not new. A search on Google will show how the literary world is full of accusations of plagiarism but it is something to be avoided. While you are at university, you need to become aware of the potential implications of plagiarism and learn to avoid any of the common mistakes which can lead to suspicion that the work you submit for marking is not your own.

There are steps everyone can take to avoid accusations of plagiarism. Digital environments offer a quick and easy facility for copying and pasting text from one place to another. This means it is easy to use a variety of different online sources when you are compiling notes or writing an assignment. The most common error students make, in particular at the start of their course, is to copy and paste passages of text from the internet without citing the source. This can make it look as though you are presenting your own work rather than the work of someone else. The charge of plagiarism can be avoided by correct referencing. This means that every time you refer to the work of another person, you need to make an explicit reference to the original source. This is most commonly done in an abbreviated form within the text. For example, if you were to refer to this book you would reference it within the text as (Watling and Rogers, 2012) and with full details in your list of references at the end. A full reference commonly includes the author(s) names(s), the date of publication, the title of the work and the details of the journal or the publisher. Following the example given above, if you were to reference this book it would appear in your list of references as follows:

Watling, S and Rogers, J (2012) *Social Work in a Digital Society*. Exeter: Learning Matters.

Correct referencing means anyone reading your work can go to the original source and find the document you have used. There are a number of different referencing systems used within difference disciplines. A common system within social science is the 'Harvard' system but your own school or department may have their own preference. It is important to ensure you know which system to use and your library will be able to give you advice on the one which is most appropriate for your course.

RESEARCH SUMMARY

Ctrl + V = plagiarism

Intentional plagiarism is an act of fraud, but it can happen through misunderstanding the need for accurate citation or referencing. Universities are increasingly using plagiarism detection software which looks for matches between your text and existing content on the internet. If a substantial match is found, with no accreditation, you may find yourself being called in for interview and further explanation. If your school or department uses plagiarism detection software, staff may encourage you to submit your assignments through the checking process. This can be a useful exercise for your own peace of mind, even if it is not a compulsory part of the submission procedure. To avoid accidental plagiarism, make sure you are familiar with referencing requirements. When you are making notes, write down the full reference details of every source of information, including the website address if the content is online. Be clear about the distinction between your ideas and those of your reference sources; using coloured highlights can help. Another cause of unintentional plagiarism is poor time management. Students panic and feel that using other people's work is preferable to a late submission. This is an incorrect assumption. Remember your tutors are experienced markers and will spot anything suspicious in your work such as a change of text style or a sense that they have read something similar elsewhere. Think of plagiarism as theft. It is one of the most serious academic offences you can commit while at university but also one of the easiest to avoid. Visit the internet Detective at www.vts.intute.ac.uk/detective. This online activity supports using the internet for research and emphasises the importance of correct referencing in order to avoid suspicions of plagiarism.

Digital literacies

Effective use of the internet for education and for professional practice involves adopting the appropriate digital literacies. Digital literacies include the ways you work within digital environments and management of digital content, but as the internet increasingly supports social interaction, being digitally literate also includes the ways in which you present yourself online. This online identity includes the information which might be returned if a prospective employer were to key your name into Google. It is worth doing this yourself to check what comes up. You may be surprised at just how much information is publicly available. In Chapter 1 we looked at the difference between private and public online identities and the importance of maintaining a line between personal and professional online behaviours. In Chapter 6 there is further information about what it means to be a digitally literate student and practitioner in a digital age.

Digital cognition

Some researchers are saying that the shift to digital text is changing the way in which information is being read and absorbed. The idea of the medium affecting brain functions is not new. In the fourth century BC, the Greek philosopher Socrates was critical about the development of writing. Socrates feared that it was becoming a replacement for the oral tradition of spoken knowledge. He believed that if society became dependent on the written word, citizens would no longer exercise their memory and would become forgetful. Similar concerns were expressed following the invention of the Gutenberg printing press in the late fifteenth century, which enabled the mass production and distribution of text for the first time. In 1477, an Italian book editor named Hieronimo Squarciafico expressed concern that an abundance of books might make people less inclined to study, resulting in a weakening of the mind. We may find these ideas old-fashioned or amusing in the twenty-first century, but there has been research which suggests that exposure to digital content is affecting the way in which we read, in particular changing the neural mechanisms through which we absorb and process information. The concept of a 'changing brain' was noted by the German philosopher Friedrich Nietzsche in the late nineteenth century. When he started to lose his eyesight, Nietzsche bought himself a typewriter and learned to touch type. A friend later commented on how his style of writing had changed, observing that it had become less fluid and more precise. Nietzsche's experience demonstrates the way in which communication channels may influence self-expression. The phrase 'the Google generation' is often used to refer to those born after 1993 who have grown up in an internet-enabled society where a keyboard is more common than pen and paper. In 2008 research into the ways in which young people search for information on the internet suggested that they were operating differently in virtual environments, in particular when it came to evaluating content (British Library and JISC, 2008). Researchers found that while participants appeared confident with digital technology, this was often at the expense of competence. Searching behaviours included impatient 'surface' level approaches which sought instant answers. Horizontal rather than vertical research techniques were favoured and the speed with which links were selected left little time for looking at key academic issues such as relevance, accuracy or authority.

. . . they scan, flick and 'power browse' their way through digital content, developing new forms of online reading on the way that we do not yet fully understand.

(British Library and JISC, 2008, p8)

The proliferation of hyperlinks on a web page can serve as a continual interruption, resulting in concentration becoming scattered across a range of unrelated areas and making it difficult to focus on a single issue. Ongoing distractions mean that although we think we know where we are headed, we often end up somewhere completely different from where we first began. Does this sound familiar? The processes of successful learning involve exactly the opposite approach. To learn effectively we need to pause and reflect. It is this process of internalisation, of linking new knowledge with existing experience, which forms the basis of reflective practice and helps to turn surface learning into deep learning. Deep learning not only lies at the heart of the higher education experience but also is essential for critical reflective practice, which is integral to social work. Being reflective slows down the learning experience. It requires time to process and reprocess your ideas; the exact opposite of the effect which current research suggests the internet is having on us all.

CHAPTER SUMMARY

- Social work education has a dual purpose to support development of appropriate digital literacies and to equip students with critical awareness of the social impact of the internet and digital divides. It offers a safe and supportive environment in which to learn about appropriate digital behaviours which can then be transferred to professional working practice.

- The affordances of the internet and Web 2.0 technologies offer students a range of opportunities for engagement with digital environments and the development of the necessary transferable skills required for professional practice in the twenty-first century.

- The social work curriculum is designed to support students who can positively engage with digital literacies, help them develop the prerequisite confidence and competence and gain a full understanding of the implications of digital ways of working within their chosen profession.

FURTHER READING

Carr, N (2008) Is Google making us stupid? *The Atlantic*, July/August. Available online at www.theatlantic.com/magazine/archive/2008/07/is-google-making-us-stupid/6868/

This short article is a useful introduction to some of the research which suggests that the internet is affecting the way in which the neural networks in the brain process information.

Cottrell, S (2003) *The study skills handbook*. Basingstoke: Palgrave Macmillan.

An essential guide to studying within higher education and developing a learning strategy which is applicable to both digital and non-digital ways of working.

Gregor, C (2006) *Practical computer skills for social work*. Exeter: Learning Matters.

This book was designed to support the growing need for social work students to engage with information and communication technologies (ICT). Written prior to the revised subject benchmarks which extended the ICT criteria to include the social impact of the internet it remains a useful revision resource for ICT basics.

Knott, C and Scragg, T (2010) *Reflective practice in social work*. Second edition. Exeter: Learning Matters.

Reflective practice is key to social work education and this book contains relevant information about the nature of reflection as well as case studies which demonstrate the application of theory to practice.

USEFUL WEBSITES

Intute A free online service providing a gateway to finding content relevant to social welfare and social work. Available at www.intute.ac.uk

Virtual Training Suite for social work A useful set of free, online tutorials offering guidance for using the internet to find information for coursework and assignments. Available at www.vts.intute.ac.uk/tutorial/socialwork

The Internet Detective An interactive learning experience covering ways of establishing the authenticity of online content and advice on how to avoid suspicion of plagiarism though the use of correct referencing. Available at www.vts.intute.ac.uk/detective

Social Care Institute for Excellence (SCIE) Online learning resources which include an extensive range of multimedia content on health and social care issues in the UK. Available at www.scie.org.uk

Chapter 5

Social work placements and practice in a digital age

How people engage with and are perceived by the services and systems they encounter is increasingly shaped by information technology.

(Hardy and Loader, 2009, p660)

Unless social workers do become involved in the ways in which new technologies are used within organisations, they will fail to influence its impact on their clients and may further fail to control the way in which computers affect the nature of social work itself in the future.

(Sapey, 1997, p803)

ACHIEVING A SOCIAL WORK DEGREE

This chapter will help you to develop the following capabilities, to the appropriate level, from the Social Work Professional Capabilities Framework.

- **Professionalism.** Identify and behave as a professional social worker committed to professional development.
- **Values and ethics.** Apply social work ethical principles and values to guide professional practice.
- **Diversity.** Recognise diversity and apply anti-discriminatory and anti-oppressive principles in practice.
- **Justice.** Advance human rights and promote social justice and economic well-being.
- **Knowledge.** Apply knowledge of social sciences, law and social work practice theory.
- **Judgement.** Use judgement and authority to intervene with individuals, families and communities to promote independence, provide support and prevent harm, neglect and abuse.
- **Critical reflection and analysis.** Apply critical reflection and analysis to inform and provide a rationale for professional decision-making.
- **Contexts and organisations.** Engage with, inform, and adapt to changing contexts that shape practice.

See Appendix 1 for the Professional Capabilities Framework diagram.

The chapter will also introduce you to the following academic standards as set out in the 2008 Social Work Subject Benchmark statement:

5.1.1 **Social work services, service users and carers.**
5.1.2 **The service delivery context.**
5.1.5 **The nature of social work practice.**
5.9 **ICT and numerical skills.**

Introduction

When you go on to placement or into employment in social work it is likely that you will be in an office or space in which screens and computers outnumber people. To organise, deliver and account for social work practice in today's world requires significant use of digital technologies for the purposes of recording and sharing data and information. These technologies are changing social work practice, often rapidly and in significant ways. In this chapter we will examine some examples of this. Although it can seem that the digital landscape is changing at a dizzying pace, the aim is for this material to prepare you for some of the ways digital technologies are actually used in practice settings. By practice settings we mean local authorities, other statutory agencies and the whole range of third-sector agencies in which practitioners work. We hope this will give you a reasonable understanding of some of the opportunities and problems the introduction of electronic information systems and other digital technologies can bring to social work practice. The implications for social workers and their managers, and also for service users, will be considered. We will also build on material from Chapter 4 and address some of the ways technologies are being used to enhance the practice-based elements of social work education, such as examples of virtual workplaces and environments and tools which are being used to enhance the placement learning experience for students.

It is likely that you are also a personal user of digital technologies of various kinds. You may have a personal mobile phone with you when on placement; you may use Facebook, or Twitter, and be accustomed to communicating with friends and family in various digital ways throughout the day. This chapter will provide some guidance on the appropriate use of both personal devices and systems and agency technologies and systems when you are a student or employee.

Skills for Care, an organisation which is tasked with developing the social care workforce to meet anticipated demands, published a workforce strategy in 2011 (Skills for Care, 2011). The strategy makes specific reference to some of the digital technologies we consider in this chapter, including social media, assistive technology and circles of support. It suggests the effective use of technology requires skills in:

- assessing the benefits of technological support to promote autonomy;

- offering appropriate guidance to enable people to gain access to information relating to assistive technologies as and when they want it;

- enabling people who use services, carers and people in their circles of support to understand assistive technology and ensuring they are enabled to use it with confidence;

- social networking to support local leaders and providers to use web-based applications to engage with the public and the communities they serve;

- supporting the use of social media;

- learning and sharing knowledge through technology, using e-learning resources as part of continuing professional development.

Familiarity with the Skills for Care strategy, along with the National Occupational Standards for Social Work and the new Professional Capabilities Framework for Social Work which has been developed by the Social Work Reform Board, will give you a good sense of the knowledge and skills which will be required by social workers in the coming years in relation to new digital technologies. Material in this chapter is aimed at assisting this process.

Technology and social work placements

In Chapter 4 we covered the use of digital technologies within educational settings. Some of the systems, resources and technologies which you use within the university setting will of course continue to feature in your education and experience as you move into placements. Next, we focus on some specific examples of the use of technologies to assist and enhance the learning experience within social work placements, before examining a range of examples of and debates about technologies at work in different areas of social work practice.

The use of virtual reality in training and practice

There are now a number of examples of virtual reality being used as an educational tool. You may be familiar with *Second Life*, a three-dimensional online virtual world. Users are able to develop an avatar, which is a three-dimensional graphical representation of themselves, and to then interact with others in many ways in a virtual world. *Second Life* is a very popular leisure activity with over 20 million registered users. To give just one example of the educational potential for social work training, *Second Life* was used to assist in the development of courtroom skills at the School of Health and Social Science at the University of Wales (Morris and Andrews, 2011). Real courtrooms and practitioners are expensive to hire and the use of a virtual courtroom offered students a chance to prepare and deliver court reports in a simulated environment which gave a better sense of the reality of legal proceedings than exercises in a university classroom.

At Greenwich University students developed a virtual environment which allowed them to interact with service users online. Home visits could be simulated and trainee social workers asked to make decisions based on the events that unfold on screen. Developed by their Centre for Research with Fragile Families, the scenarios allowed trainees to send an avatar to encounter potentially difficult or dangerous situations with families with children who may be at risk of harm.

More recently in the USA, one university has begun to use a virtual environment in the training of social workers to help treat post-traumatic stress disorder. Again developed from a video game, *Virtual Iraq* is being used to recreate environments in which trauma was experienced and to train students to work with returning soldiers to help them deal with traumas and other symptoms (Halpern, 2008).

Some educational institutions have recognised the benefits of technologies in managing placements for students. Systems such as LeaRNS, an administrative system recommended by the General Social Care Council (GSCC), Skills for Care and others have been used for matching students and placements. This was a web-based system, developed by Skills for

Care with the aim of supporting professional development at all levels. However, at the time of writing this book, The College of Social Work announced that financially supporting LeaRNS would no longer be viable for a number of reasons, including costs and prospective changes to the way in which the Social Work Education Group would be managed in the future. Skills for Care concluded that there was no other option but to close the LeaRNS project during 2012. This example demonstrates some of the sustainability issues of working with digital environments and how changing times can result in the closure of systems.

During your placements you will become familiar with another system, the national Quality Assurance for Practice Learning (QAPL) and you will be expected to complete feedback on your placement as part of this process. There were plans for this to be integrated into the LeaRNS system so that students completed their feedback electronically and, although the demise of LeaRNS has been announced, the move towards digitising student response to placement will inevitably be progressed.

More useful, from a student perspective, are moves to use electronic systems to provide more than electronic forms. Online forums and real-time discussions between students, academics, placements staff and practice educators, for example, have been used with success in some areas.

Digital stories

Later in this chapter we discuss concerns that a digital database culture is taking over from a narrative-based culture within welfare services. During the same period in which these concerns have been widely expressed, and information about users of services has increasingly been shaped by the digital technology systems which are used to hold and disseminate that information, there has also been increasing emphasis on listening to the voice and experience of the service user. As you will be aware from your course of study, and perhaps from experience, the ways in which service users can be involved in services and in education are many and varied. One approach which has been successfully used in educational settings and which allows for a holistic narrative or story to be communicated is via the use of digital stories. Here, rather than constraining or dissecting narrative within a database framework, the technology allows for the encapsulation and communication of a narrative which has emotional impact.

In the UK, digital stories were introduced to a wider audience via national broadcasters. The BBC in conjunction with the University of Cardiff produced a set of digital stories in 2001 – the Capture Wales project. The following year the Telling Lives programme followed in England. A wide range of short film clips were available including experiences about being young and in the 'care system'. The Capture Wales videos can still be accessed online and are available at www.bbc.co.uk/wales/arts/yourvideo/queries/capture-wales.shtml. Unfortunately the BBC have made the Telling Lives videos unavailable due to the quality of the online video which it says no longer meets current technical standards. This does raise important issues about the sustainability of digital materials and should you become involved in the production of digital narratives it is worth bearing in mind how to ensure your valuable content can be best preserved.

Just as the BBC pioneered their digital stories in Wales, MIND have introduced, in 2011, a set of digital stories about experiences of mental distress, on their MIND Welsh website at www.mind.org.uk/mind_cymru. The stories have been produced in conjunction with StoryWorks, an organisation based at the Welsh Institute for Health and Social Care which was set up to help public service organisations use people's stories to improve what they do.

Also on the theme of mental health, the Centre for Excellence in Interdisciplinary Mental Health at the University of Birmingham have produced a very informative and engaging set of digital stories at www.ceimh.bham.ac.uk/tv/DigitalStoriesIntro.shtml.

In 2003 Pip Hardy and Tony Morris developed a social enterprise called Patient Voices in which a major aim was to capture and facilitate the hearing of some of the many unspoken and unwritten stories of experiences of public care. The result has been a set of experiences of both health and social care gathered together in the Patient Voices programme. The resources have been widely and freely distributed and can be viewed at www.patientvoices.org.uk.

The viewing of digital stories can be useful for your own education. You may also consider getting involved in the production of them. The technologies for doing so are widely available to educational institutions. They can provide a powerful tool for enabling social work practice which can help those who are disadvantaged to articulate and share their experiences.

Cyberethics, good practice and the use of digital technology

The following section gives some specific guidance in relation to your use of a range of digital technologies while you are on a social work placement.

Social networking

Social networking sites such as Facebook or Twitter are increasingly popular and many students use them on a regular basis. Such sites offer the facility to freely share thoughts and opinions with a very wide public. You need to think carefully about the information that you post on such sites.

Consider the following questions.

- When you are on placement you find that you do not get on with your practice assessor. Is it OK to tell your friends this on Facebook?

- If you find one of the service users really difficult, is it OK to say so on Facebook?

- Should you mention anything about your placement on Facebook?

- Should there be any other restrictions on what you say on Facebook?

Facebook claims to have over 500 million users worldwide (as at summer 2010). It is now a very common way of keeping in touch with family and friends. Many students have been using Facebook on a regular basis since before coming to university and continue to do so while they are studying social work. You might be one of them. Do you know who also shares access to your Facebook information? Even if you set the highest privacy settings certain information can be viewed by everyone using the service. You may also be sharing information with other people who have less concern about privacy than you. It may seem obvious that you should not use Facebook or Twitter to make derogatory statements about other people, especially ones that you are involved with in your role as social worker in training. However, there are several documented examples of social work students doing just this. You might be tempted to discuss online what you think are harmless or even positive aspects about your placement and people within it. This is potentially a breach of confidentiality. It can also have significant repercussions for you. Significant developments in 2011 highlighted the legal liability which users of Twitter may face when posting what they believe to be anonymous comments (Rosenberg, 2011). To avoid any confusion most training courses suggest that students *should not under any circumstances* access and use social networking sites to discuss any aspect of their practice learning opportunity (PLO) experience, agency staff, service users or the agency in which the PLO is being undertaken. In terms of other restrictions you might want to think about the professional image you should be portraying. People form their own theories about your competence, character, and commitment to being a professional worker from the way in which you present yourself. This includes what you say and the images you display on Facebook and other social networking sites. It also needs to be borne in mind that training to be a social worker requires that all students conduct themselves at all times and in all circumstances in a manner that is compliant with GSCC Registration and Codes of Conduct as well as within the policies and procedures of the agency within which they are placed. At the time of writing further evidence has emerged that even experienced professionals are not thinking carefully enough about their use of social media. Within a week, there were two separate incidents within our nearby local authority of teachers being suspended after posting derogatory comments about pupils on social networking sites (*Yorkshire Post*, 2011).

Beyond your own use of social media, it is crucial that, as a trainee social worker, you develop a broad awareness of the different ways social media are being used in the wider society. Rapid developments in this area are posing some very specific challenges for some core areas of social work, as the following case study vividly highlights.

CASE STUDY

Adopted children and contact with birth parents via Facebook

Frank is a known paedophile and has recently been released from prison. His daughter was removed from the family by social services ten years ago. Sharon is now 16 years old. Frank uses the Facebook site and recently simply typed in the name and date of birth of his daughter. He quickly found her and sent her a message, via Facebook: 'Hello. I am your father. You were taken away from me when you were a baby and I have never

Continued

stopped looking for you. I'm sure you've been told lots of things about me which aren't true. I love you and want to meet you to put the record straight.' After this, Sharon became depressed, stopped attending school, and relationships with her adoptive parents have become very difficult. Sharon's parents know about the abuse Sharon experienced as a baby and are anxious to protect her but are now feeling pressured into agreeing to some sort of formal contact.

The rise in social media networking sites such as Facebook is making it more difficult to guarantee confidentiality to adoptive parents and their children (Macdonald 2010). Adoption agencies have been reporting an increased number of calls from adoptive parents whose children have been contacted out of the blue by their birth parents. This is challenging assumptions that children's access to their birth parents is controlled until adulthood and agencies are having to deal with the consequences of online communication which is unexpected and intrusive. Given the widespread and increasing use of Facebook, it is unlikely that either legislation or policing can stop this so it is important to recognise the potential for trauma and be able to offer appropriate support and training to those involved, including children, parents and social workers.

Using computers on placement

Should you use the computer at your placement for your personal business at any time? Most agencies now use database systems to record information about service users. The use of portable data memory sticks is commonplace. Many people have home computers or carry laptops around with them. What issues does this portability of personal information raise about service user confidentiality?

As we have seen, a social worker's role has increasingly come to include administrative tasks that require you to competently use digital technologies. These might include working out financial contributions for care services, entering information on database systems, writing reports and compiling presentations. Agencies often have their own policies about the use of computers. In smaller agencies these may not be written down but you should check with your practice assessor what the expectations are. In general agency computers are intended for work undertaken on behalf of the agency. You will need to check whether it is acceptable to use the agency's computer for your portfolio-related tasks. Whatever the agency rules, however, it may be your university's view that you should not use the agency computers for personal matters, such as booking holidays, accessing websites that are not related to your placement, or for entering social networking sites.

Computers and confidentiality

You should always be aware of the storage and portability of information held on memory sticks and while this may be appropriate during the placement, once the placement has finished all work should be deleted before leaving the agency. Personal data about people which is held in digital records should ideally be encrypted. This is good practice, though it is recognised that this situation is by no means widespread. Your agency should have a policy about this, and ideally the technology to implement encryption. You should familiarise yourself with relevant data protection and freedom of information legislation. The social work and law textbooks that are recommended on your programme will have details.

Use of mobile phones including camera phones

The use of mobile phones has become part of everyday life for many people and you may be used to using your phone on a frequent basis to keep in contact with family and friends. However, when you are on placement you should enquire about the agency policy on the use of personal mobile phones. Generally the only telephone number that should be given to service users is the number of the agency concerned and under no circumstances should personal telephone details such as landline or mobile numbers be given to service users.

Here is an example of a social care agency's guidelines on the use of personal mobile phones:

- Personal phone calls/texts must not be made or received while delivering direct care or support to a service user.

- Personal phone calls/texts must not be made or received while attending meetings, reviews, supervision or similar.

- Personal phone calls/texts at other times must not interfere with the staff member's duties.

- Making or receiving personal phone calls or texts while at work can undermine the principle of respect for service users.

However, the Community Care Service recognises that it can be useful for staff to be in mobile phone contact while at work, either because they have vulnerable dependants or because they are lone working.

The use of camera phones has also come under scrutiny since the case of Vanessa George who took indecent pictures of children in her care at a nursery (Lombard, 2009). Some agencies that work with young children have now restricted the taking of camera phones into the workplace.

As you can see, the use of information and communication technology raises many issues relating to your practice with service users while on placement. There are some simple rules you should follow:

- Ask your practice assessor for the agency's policies on the use of digital technologies and abide by these rules.

- Where no policies exist discuss the issues with your practice assessor and make a written agreement about what you should do.

- If you are unclear what you should do in a particular situation seek advice from your practice assessor.

Assistance for newly qualified social workers (NQSW)

You will be aware that since 2009 newly qualified social workers have been given a particular status. Protected caseloads, greater supervision and more access to training are some of the key aims of this move. The Skills for Care website has a useful section dedicated to resources for newly qualified social workers. A resource pack can be downloaded free from the site and included in it is an action learning programme. There is also a secure discussion forum within the site for new social workers to share thoughts, concerns and experiences. Go to the Skills for Care website at www.skillsforcare.org.uk and search for newly qualified social worker. For those working in children and family services the Children's Workforce Development Council also provide a set of useful documents and resources relating to newly qualified social workers all in one place on their website. Go to www.cwdcouncil.org.uk and search for nqsw.

Community Care, the magazine for social workers, has a sizeable website with a section devoted to NQSW where you will find useful guidance from colleagues and managers. Go to www.communitycare.co.uk and search for nqsw.

Technology and continuing professional development (CPD)

Whether you are a student on placement, newly qualified or established in practice and wishing to continue with professional development, there are a number of useful electronic resources which are freely available and will assist with the development of knowledge and skills. Technology can help in this way with access to education and training materials, such as online documents and interactive learning materials. This can also help in learning *about* technology and the ways in which technologies can aid working life for social workers and can improve experiences and outcomes for service users. The message in this book is for social workers not to take internet access for granted so, while using the internet for your own education and training purposes, you need to be constantly asking yourself whether everyone could access these resources, in particulate multimedia, or if there are any barriers to access such as MP3 audio files with no transcripts and videos which have no subtitles, captions or any textual equivalents. Refer to Chapter 3 for more details about digital equalities and digital divides and the inclusion and exclusion binary.

You will be familiar with the SCIE. They have a website at www.scie.org.uk where they maintain a wide range of up-to-date resources on all aspects of social work with multimedia and interactive electronic resources to aid learning and professional development.

The Telecare Learning and Improvement Network provides online access to regular newsletters, journal articles and other useful resources for this rapidly developing area on their website at www.telecarelin.org.uk.

The recently established College of Social Work are developing useful resources for practitioners at www.collegeofsocialwork.org.

A useful directory of websites and online resources including video tutorials is available at www.intute.ac.uk. Funding was not available to develop this resource after 2011 but existing resources will remain available.

Community Care magazine has some interesting blogs and forums on its website. Their Carespace Forum has proved a useful space for debate and for practitioners to share information and assist each other remotely. Go to www.communitycare.co.uk and look for the link to the Care Space Forum.

In Scotland a useful resource has been developed called Social Services Work Knowledge Scotland at www.ssks.org.uk. This contains materials useful to social workers across the UK. Advice on digital literacy and social media, as well as more traditional online documents, can be found. This portal also provides gateways and resources for developing online communities of practice and online networking for social care workers.

So far we have discussed issues of digital technology in relation to the educational process, whether in placements or as part of continuing professional development. Next we turn to some more general issues which are pertinent to social work practice.

Social work practice and the dominance of digital technology

A number of authors have pointed to the problems and dangers of forms of social work and other welfare services which are increasingly dominated by digital technology systems.

When the arguments against such systems are examined it is clear that often it is not the technology itself that is objected to. There are two developments which have led to the use of computer systems in ways which many social workers resist. First, a dominant style in the implementation and delivery of welfare services is one of managerialism, and a move towards attempting to reduce costs by making welfare systems more efficient and accountable through tight monitoring of activity. Second, is the fact that computer-based systems increasingly facilitate this process by making it easier to gather, analyse and share large amounts of data quickly. Social workers object, then, to the use of digital technologies predominantly for recording data in ways which are not of their choosing and for purposes which are often seen as not important for enhancing the experiences of service users. They may also question the validity of the assumption that tight monitoring of activity leads to a more efficient and effective service.

There are a number of critical social work texts which seriously question the value and efficacy of the increase in managerialism in social work, the linked focus on targets, on monitoring and recording, and the use of centralised computer systems. The perception is that these systems have taken social work away from its real task as a relationship-based human activity (Jordan, 2001; Ferguson and Woodward, 2009; Rogowski, 2010). It has been suggested that such developments may lead to a *diversion of resources to technology, software, consultants and technicians and the curtailment of client choice due to procedures required by electronic recording formats and pro-forma* (Burton and Van Den Broek, 2009, p1327).

In an influential paper for the *British Journal of Social Work*, Parton (2008) suggested that social work had moved from an activity based on 'relational' knowledge to one based on 'informational' knowledge. He develops an idea expressed by Manovich (2001) that the database, originally a method for organising and accessing data, has *become the privileged form of cultural expression* (Parton, 2008, p261). This idea contrasts a database mentality with a narrative mentality which was previously the prevailing form of cultural expression, and of practice in welfare services. Indeed until recently social work practice relied on the construction of narratives based on interviews and the conversion of oral into written information. As we shall see in the following examples, the change to a database culture dominated by the recording of many bits of information in standardised forms and systems has a number of consequences, many of which do not facilitate the best outcomes for services users or workers within welfare services. This has been recognised by many authors, and government reports on the future of social work are now advocating a return to recording systems which allow more narrative flow (Munro, 2011).

The next section examines some specific examples of the impact of digital technologies within different areas of social work practice, illustrating some of the problems and advantages which reliance on digital technologies can open up. We begin with several examples from children and family services. This is an area which, perhaps more than any other area of social work, has been subject to a raft of computer-based recording and monitoring systems.

Children and family services

Over many years a number of inquiries into non-accidental child deaths in the UK have produced findings which criticise and implicate deficiencies in information sharing between agencies. From a different perspective the duplication of assessments and records by a range of different agencies is viewed as inefficient and wasteful of public resources. Both of these drivers have led to demands for more centralised electronic systems for recording information and sharing it between different public agencies, with the suggestion that such developments will improve the safeguarding of vulnerable children.

Ironically, as we will see, recent evidence and commentaries have suggested that the very information and monitoring procedures which have been introduced with the intention of improving safety may in fact lead to a greater number of errors and not achieve the better outcomes for vulnerable people they were designed to achieve (Munro, 2011).

You will be familiar with the cases of both Victoria Climbié and of Baby Peter. The former led to the most significant reform to social work with children and families since the 1960s. This was signified by *Every Child Matters* (ECM), a government programme of reform which led to new law in the shape of The Children's Act 2004. Alongside this, several significant developments involving digital technologies have been occurring, and as White et al. (2009) have noted, ECM has relied significantly on an e-government agenda to support some of its ambitions (e-government meaning the use of electronic means to record, share and communicate information relevant to government). The Baby Peter tragedy led to further reforms, developed by a task force and a reform board whose recommendations were accepted by government and led to changes, from 2011 onwards, in the structure of the social work degree programme, in the nature and length of placements and in workplace and managerial practices.

The Common Assessment Framework (CAF)

One response to the drivers for greater and more efficient recording and sharing of information in relation to children who may be at risk was the development of the Common Assessment Framework (CAF), introduced in 2006. The government saw this as a key part of delivering front-line services that are integrated and focused around the needs of children and young people (Department for Education and Skills, 2007). After much discussion an electronic version of this, e-CAF, was introduced in 2010. Funded by the Department for Education, a single national system began to be tested with a limited number of organisations. After a period of consultation, ministers have decided to decommission e-CAF in 2012. This decision aligns with the view of Professor Munro that the prescription of national information technology systems can be constraining to local innovation and professional judgement, and so should be removed. This is another example of a government-supported digital system being introduced and then withdrawn as not fit for purpose.

The Information Sharing and Assessment project (ISA) was another aspect of the ECM agenda. The aim was to ensure that any child who was vulnerable or at risk was referred to appropriate services. Local authorities developed ISA teams and strategies to develop mechanisms for delivering better recording and sharing of information. These almost always involved significant technical expertise in relation to digital technologies and systems. Again the intention of using digital technologies as a central part of this programme was clear.

ContactPoint

One of the most controversial aspects of this programme of developments was the construction of a comprehensive database, containing the details of all 11 million children in the UK and made accessible to appropriate professionals for them to be able to record concerns about children and any involvement they had with a particular child. This became known as ContactPoint. From 2004 onwards there were strong objections to and criticisms of this database from professionals, academics, the media and parliamentary scrutineers (Pithouse et al., 2009). It was variously seen as authoritarian, expensive, intrusive, unreliable and beset with risks of large amounts of data falling into the wrong hands. The new coalition government scrapped the scheme and the database was turned off in August 2010. The story of ContactPoint highlights once again the problems of striking an equitable and appropriate balance between the needs and benefits of digital information sharing on a wide scale and the loss of confidentiality, privacy and civil rights which may ensue from this.

The Integrated Children's System

Another instructive example concerning the use of digital technologies and information systems in this area of practice is that of the Integrated Children's System (ICS), a development which has been the object of significant commentary and debate. While noting the potential benefits of standardised and centralised recording systems, most published evaluations of ICS have concluded that it is far from 'fit for purpose' (White et al., 2009). For example, when asked for their views about the operation of the system, social workers typically reported that *the tick boxes were often irrelevant and too imprecise to be useful, the forms were too complex to share with families, children and other professionals* and *none contained a first person statement by a service user* (Shaw et al., 2009, p619).

After many complaints about the rigidity of ICS, a ministerial communication in 2009 reminded local authorities that it was not a rigid system imposed by government; rather that local authorities should *determine how ICT systems can be used to support the delivery of social care services. The key test of those systems should be that they support effective practice and improved outcomes for children, young people and their families* (Department for Children, Schools and Families, 2009, p21).

ICT was one of the specific areas that Eileen Munro was asked to look at in her 2010 review of child protection systems in England and Wales (Munro, 2011). Noting that the ICS system has been problematic she suggests that with ICS *the degree of standardisation imposed by the current system may be supportive to novices but is not likely to enhance professional learning and skill and indeed may erode its development* (Munro, 2011, p58).

She noted that information and communication technology systems are experienced as unhelpful in two ways. Social workers are required to spend too much time completing digital documentation and ICS does not help enough in the creation of chronologies and the child's story. Crucially, Munro notes that *Accordingly, the matter of technology cannot be separated from the practice model, nor from the inspectorial and performance management systems* (Munro, 2011, pp59–60). This is an important point. Large digital information and communication systems are often imposed upon public services and practitioners, who are forced to interact with them, having little, if any, say in their design and development. The purpose may be more related to monitoring performance than to improving the service for the end user or the practitioner. Those systems often do not meet the needs of the users and furthermore are often prone to technical faults. Many social workers who made contributions to the Munro Review noted that locally procured computer systems in local authorities often posed substantial obstacles to good practice (Munro, 2011).

For digital technologies to be most useful end users, including the users of public services, their families and professionals who work with them, should have some input into their development and implementation. In fact this is a point which is applicable not only to digital technologies but also to the whole operation of public services, and their systems of delivery. John Seddon (2008) has written eloquently about the waste which results when services are designed from the top down. He gives many examples of ways in which applying systems thinking, and designing systems from the starting point of the needs of the end user, can lead to real efficiencies and lower costs. He argues that digital technologies which are often bought to implement command and control systems in public services can actually design in poor service and higher costs. In this view digital technologies are simply one part of a wider set of tools and systems which are used to deliver and monitor public services in a particular way and one which may not be particularly efficient or effective.

In relation to social work, detailed research with Australian practitioners regarding the impact of digital technologies and computer-based information systems suggested that *social workers should be more adequately integrated into the design and application of the technology with commensurate on-going training on such systems* (Burton and Van Den Broek, 2009, p1329). Specifically in relation to the arena of social work with children and families, Munro (2011) has suggested that future ICT systems should make full use of multimedia. She recommends that users, including children and young people and their carers, should be involved in designing such systems and that items such as photographs and digital stories could be made use of more widely. This would help to counter the tendency of digitally based recording systems to lose sight of the human individual and their life story in a mass of tick boxes and disjointed text. Her review highlights this issue as a major challenge and suggests an urgent need to develop, with the input of social workers, new systems to meet their case recording needs. She also suggests that this should be a locally driven initiative rather than a central imposition and that in procuring any new software local authorities should pay close attention to the following three principles.

- Recording systems for child and family social work should meet the critical need to maintain a systemic and family narrative, which describes all the events associated with the interaction between a social worker, other professionals and the child and their family.

- ICT systems for child and family social work should be able to adapt with relative ease to changes in local child protection system needs, operational structures and data performance requirements.

- The analysis of requirements for ICT-based systems for child and family social work should primarily be based on a human-centred analysis of what is required by front-line workers; any clashes between the functional requirements that have been identified by this process and those associated with management information reporting should normally be resolved in terms of the former.

(Munro, 2011, p111)

RESEARCH SUMMARY

Research by Burton and Van Den Broek (2009) in an Australian context illustrated clearly how some of the ways in which digital technologies are being used is leading to social workers focusing less on professional values and professional accountability for practice, and more on bureacratic accountabilities. In the UK context, a paper by Pithouse et al. (2009) critically explored the impact on practice of the introduction of the electronic Common Assessment Framework. One year later a critical assessment of a number of the digital systems that we have discussed in relation to children and family social work was published by Hall et al. (2010).

ACTIVITY **5.1**

Visit the department of education website at www.education.gov.uk and search for the Common Assessment Framework forms and guidance for practitioners. Look carefully at the whole of the assessment form and the guidance notes. What do you think are the advantages and limitations of this form?

COMMENT

Social work with children and families has come to be seen by policymakers and many managers as increasingly a matter of managing risk and dangerousness. One consequence has been the increasing use of detailed recording and monitoring systems, such as the Common Assessment Framework (CAF), which require social workers to spend a great deal of time in entering information into computer systems. To counterbalance this it should be noted that ICTs can improve the sharing of information between individuals and agencies, reduce the need for repetitive recording and provide a range of benefits to both social workers and users of services.

CASE STUDY

Mobile technology for social workers

In 2010, looking for new and more efficient ways of working, Gateshead Council introduced new mobile technologies for the social workers in their children's department. By the end of 2010, 53 tablet-style computers had been given out to staff. The tablets were fit for the purpose of storing sensitive information and equipped with full data encryption for safe storage on the move. It is reported that they have also proved a huge hit with workers. After initial concerns about workers spending more time with the technology than with the client, reports suggest that the opposite is often true, as information can be both uploaded and downloaded at convenient times, there is a reduction in the duplication of information, and workers report significant time savings in relation to the completion of comprehensive assessments. Data is entered on the tablets with either a keyboard or an electronic pen, giving social workers the benefits of both tools, as well as the flexibility to use the method they prefer. Tablets are a good portable solution, attaching to docking stations either for office working or for the quick transfer of information. Equally the solution facilitates the quick downloading of materials for mobile work, such as ICS assessment forms for offline completion. While many social workers are sceptical about the amount of resources which are invested into digital technology projects and question the benefits they can bring, this example illustrates the advantages when they are carefully chosen and planned. In the case of Gateshead Council the technology is demonstrably reducing the amount of time which is spent on entering data into recording systems and concerns about security are addressed by the use of data encryption.

It should be noted that the new standards for employers of social workers includes a requirement to *Provide social workers with appropriate practical tools to do their job including effective case recording and other IT systems, access to the internet and mobile communications* (Department for Education, 2010, p26). If your placement or workplace does not provide adequate communication technologies, it is worth reminding the agency of their obligations and of how a service can be improved with investment in the appropriate systems which are fit for purpose.

Adult services: Personalisation and digital technology

One of the larger projects of recent UK governments in relation to public service is that of personalising services; meaning offering greater choice and control to those who need to use public welfare services. Moran (2003) has referred to this as one of the *grand narratives* of recent social policy. Drivers from the demands of service users for reform and a better quality of public service have converged with cultural and political shifts towards greater individualism, and led to a clear public policy of offering more choice of providers to those who use public services, and more direct control of the resources to which they are entitled.

It first became legal to make cash payments to service users under the Direct Payments Act 1996. Despite a great deal of encouragement from government the actual uptake of direct payments was slow to develop. Pilot projects of more flexible individual budgets for social care users led to national roll-out, targets of 30 per cent of eligible adult service users being in receipt of personal budgets by March 2011 and then an aspiration that all service users will be offered personal budgets by 2013. The increased personal choice which is one of the major aims of this process is of course predicated on a range of choices being accessible to service users. One way in which this can be facilitated is via the use of digital technologies. Online marketplaces, for example, can provide an accessible portal or gateway to a range of internet-based services. Again, we should be aware here of the danger of digital divides being reinforced if those with the means to access information and services digitally are at an advantage compared to those who cannot access online information and marketplaces.

As we have discussed earlier, there is the possibility of a residual service for service users who are less assertive and who are digitally excluded, in a world in which many people increasingly buy services online, and in which those with easy access to high-speed secure connections and who are confident and able with online financial transactions can get the best deals and a wider choice of deals.

One aspect of the development of personalisation is that of brokerage. Although the role is also being developed as a separate specialist role in some areas, as a social worker one of your roles may be as a broker of services, helping individuals to navigate their way around a range of services which are available to those who are entitled to support from public bodies, including local authorities and the NHS. As a broker you will need to become familiar with the growing range of services which are available to the service user whom you are helping to secure services.

A good broker may be able to help those service users who are less digitally literate to access relevant resources and services. Nevertheless it is unlikely that those who are digitally excluded, without direct, accessible and ready connections to the online marketplaces, will have the same level of choice. It should be noted at this point that the role of social work in relation to brokerage remains contested. Some service user organisations and a number of service users who took part in recent research think that brokerage should be offered only by service-user-led organisations and that local authority employed social workers inevitably have conflicts of interest (Gardner, 2011). It is at this point unclear how this debate will play out and, in practice, around the country social workers are becoming brokers and are needing to become skilled and savvy at finding a broader range of support and services that can help meet people's needs. The internet and computerised information systems may be very central in enabling a brokerage role and allowing a social worker or other enabler to assist a service user in finding out what is available and in choosing the best services from an increasing range of choices. This points to the importance of brokers developing very good digital skills and also to the fact that they will have a significant role in ensuring that service users with a range of disabilities are not excluded from digital environments which at present often present many barriers to them.

CASE STUDY

Shop4Support

This service was developed by the user-led organisation called In Control. The online service they provide is described as a citizen portal. As well as providing a 'one-stop online shop' for relevant services it is suggested that the portal can provide access to:

- *free and low-cost local groups and activities, thereby encouraging social capital;*

- *opportunities for citizens to feed back and share information about support products and services;*

- *useful council contacts;*

- *a lot of help and advice about personalisation, self-directed support and support planning.*

The service users who designed Shop4Support planned that it would be a tool for building social capital as well as simply providing information. To this end they built in features such as 'My Life', which incorporates support planning tools, 'Ask the Expert' forums and 'Shared Stories', which In Control suggest provide a useful complement to the marketplace functions. In terms of a marketplace the site offers four portals to relevant services. You can search for products and services, find a personal assistant, find local groups and activities and browse the stores. This example is highlighted in the government document, A vision for adult social care: Capable communities and active citizens (Department of Health, 2010a). Harrow Council was the first in the UK to utilise such an online marketplace of this nature when they formed a partnership in 2010 with Shop4Support. Further information can be found at www.shop4support.com. Go to the site, click for the My Council Tab at the top of the page and have a look at the information for Harrow Council. Detailed information for other local authorities

Continued

CASE STUDY *continued*

is continually appearing in this area of the site. In early 2012 15 local authorities in the Yorkshire and Humber region announced the roll-out of a new social care marketplace, beginning with Doncaster Council. Shop4support are again providing the online infra-structure for this programme. This development illustrates the rapidly expanding nature of e-marketplaces in social care. Given that the majority of social care service users will be receiving personal budgets in the future and be eligible to shop around in such market-places, it is essential that you are aware of these developments and able to assist service users in accessing and navigating these online facilities.

CASE STUDY

Payment cards and direct payments

One other way in which technology is assisting the use of direct payments is via payment cards. Kent County Council, one of the largest in the UK, was the first local authority in the UK to provide a payment card for direct payment users called the Kent Card. Developed in conjunction with the Royal Bank of Scotland, the system allows the authority to provide eligible service users who use direct payments with a card preloaded with their agreed funding amount. It gives users the autonomy and freedom that other debit cards would but without having to open accounts with financial institutions. The care manager from the local authority verifies the identity of the service user to the bank, obviating the need for a visit to the bank itself. The bank then issues the card along with a pin number and provides regular statements to the user. The user is also able to top up the card with personal funding, above that provided by their entitlement from the authority. The authority has described the use of payment cards as follows.

> On a practical level, the Pre-loaded Cards mean the recipient (or their carer) doesn't have to manage a bank account, cheque book and debit card, or to carry large amounts of cash. They simply use the card. The Pre-loaded Card also opens up the facility of Direct Payments and accounts to people who may have been excluded in the past from opening bank accounts. It also gives cardholders the opportunity to take advantage of making purchases over the internet or telephone which is particularly convenient for those care recipients with mobility issues.

(Mills, 2009)

In developing your skills for social work in modern adult services it is worth spending some time familiarising yourself with some of the increasingly diverse and digital local and national resources which are being made available to service users and for which you may become a 'broker'. Many local authorities are now providing extensive information online. We suggest that you check the web pages of your own nearest local authorities, and also look at the example of Durham County Council. Their Durham Information Guide (DIG) is a free online database which allows you to search countywide, regional and national information for social care, health and community information, such as arts, leisure, sports and social clubs and organisations. Visit the council website at www.durham.gov.uk and search for Social Care and Health and then Durham Information Guide.

Services for older people

In developments which parallel the Common Assessment Framework for children, a Single Assessment Process (SAP) was developed for older people, with a particular aim of bringing together information from the NHS and from social care providers. This development was mandated by the National Service Framework for Older People (2000).

Since older people form the largest percentage of users of social care services and many of those who use local authority social care also have many episodes of NHS care, an efficient and effective method of recording and sharing information was long overdue. The Commission for Social Care Inspection estimated in 2008 that just under 1.1 million older people used social care services in 2006 (CSCI, 2008). About four per cent of the overall older population were receiving institutional care in residential or nursing homes or long-stay hospitals, and nine per cent of that population (those aged 65 and over) received home-based care.

An electronic version of the SAP (e-SAP) was developed in 2007. Hosted centrally by British Telecom this web-based application is available to the NHS and social services and is linked to what are known as NHS Spine services. The term Spine services refers to a number of electronic health information systems, including the Choose and Book system for booking hospital and clinic appointments, an electronic prescription service and what should eventually become a national electronic patient record. Some of the same criticisms which led to the demise of ContactPoint have been levelled against the electronic patient record (known as the Summary Care Record). There are clear benefits to having a brief electronic patient record which can be accessed quickly in emergencies; for information about prescriptions and allergies, for example. However, there are technical problems relating to the compatibility of ICT systems, training issues and concerns relating to confidentiality and civil liberties (Greenhalgh et al., 2010). In relation to this it should be noted that a fairly damning report emerged from a Parliamentary Public Accounts Committee in 2011. An audit report stated clearly that the £11 billion NHS National Programme for IT would not deliver its stated aim of making a *clinically rich medical record available to local hospitals where a patient may well be treated, or making a Summary National Care Record available across England, for use when someone needs urgent treatment away from home* (BBC News, 2011).

The Parliamentary Committee were incredulous that, after spending an amount of money that could pay for half a million nurses, the programme was unlikely to deliver and was of *limited benefit* (House of Commons Committee of Public Accounts, 2010, p7). In view of this we might conclude that seamless national systems for the digital storage and communication of service user records remain a long way off. This example also invites analysis of the extent to which investment in these types of digital communication and information systems in welfare services is well planned, appropriate and cost-effective; a question which becomes ever more urgent in an era in which welfare spending is being significantly scaled back.

Telecare and assistive technologies

What has become known as telecare has become a major focus for health and social care providers in recent years. The term refers to technologies which are used to assist in providing care and support to vulnerable people (particularly older people and those with serious or chronic illness) or to those living in remote areas. The aim is often to maintain and prolong independence and to help prevent the need for a person to move into a more supervised care environment. Examples include monitoring systems, such as fall and movement sensors; mobile phone technology for monitoring of health conditions such as diabetes; and video conferencing systems that allow individuals to interact with carers, family friends and professionals, even in remote areas. The term *assistive technologies* is also used to describe products and services which are designed to enable independence. As well as those in older age groups, people of all ages with a range of physical and intellectual impairments benefit from assistive technologies. We discussed some of the issues relating to these technologies in Chapter 3.

CASE STUDY

Telecare systems

East Riding of Yorkshire Council invested in a new centre which provided a centre and hub for a number of technologies relevant to social care. The widely used Lifeline system allows users to call for assistance by pushing a button on a pendant worn round the neck. In the case of a fall, for example, this allows a user to instantly send a message to the call centre, who can then either call a relative to visit or send a member of the authority staff to visit the location from which the call was received. In East Yorkshire the system is used by thousands of service users, many of them older people at risk of falls. There are also a number of other types of users in situations with an increased potential of risk and danger, including schools, those at risk of domestic violence and employees of the authority. For example, an isolated occupational therapy equipment store was equipped with motion sensors and staff given pendants and fall sensors, in order to reduce the risk when working alone in this environment.

Increasingly the information provided by technologies such as Lifeline is being used to inform social care. For example, when conducting reviews the information that a service user or their relatives provide about their behaviour and their level of risk is not always accurate and may be different from the information provided by the log at the call centre. There is a move to use the records provided by motion and fall sensors, for example, in review processes.

In this authority, the Transformation team recently agreed that 'virtual' budgets could be used to purchase equipment to set up telecare systems, and questions about telecare have been introduced to the self-assessment questionnaires which are used by service users, in order to ensure that the technologies are considered, where relevant, when planning personalised care and considering personal budgets. The authority is working towards introducing prompts for questions about telecare in all social care assessment processes.

Telecare and assistive technologies clearly have the potential to help people to maintain independence and to improve the quality of life for them and their carers. Such benefits have been demonstrated in a number of evaluations, particularly of services for older people. A detailed evaluation of Scottish schemes, for example, indicates significant reductions in unplanned hospital admissions, delayed discharges from hospital, and care home admissions, following a large-scale telecare development programme. A saving of £48 million was estimated between 2006 and 2010, with half of the saving accruing from reductions in care home admissions (Scottish Government, 2010).

For governments faced with the simultaneous challenges of recruiting a sufficient social care work force, dealing with a rapidly ageing population, increased demands for services and pressure to reduce costs, preventative technologies such as some of those in the telecare initiative seem to offer much promise and their use looks set to accelerate.

From a social work perspective this march of technology, while holding out the promise of empowerment and increased independence for users, is not without potential problems. Fisk (2001) has suggested that telecare might promote medical models of ageing and undo some of the progress made in developing more inclusive social models (your social work training will give you an opportunity at various points to study medical and social models in different ways in relation to disability, to ageing, and to mental health). There have also been concerns about the availability of the means leading to an excessive use of surveillance technologies such as electronic tagging or tracking devices which use GPS technology to monitor movement and location. Set against this it should be noted that agencies which work with and provide support for those concerned, such as the Alzheimer's Society, have been supportive of the introduction of such technologies, recognising the need to balance risks against the scope of potential benefits (Alzheimer's Society, 2007). Moreover, studies suggest that a large majority (87 per cent) of older adults indicated that they would be *willing to give up some of my privacy* if a specific technology were able to help them remain living independently (Barrett, 2008, p8).

Returning to one of the central themes of this book, there have been those who have expressed concerns about the potential of these technologies to reinforce digital divides. It has been suggested that as remote telecare technologies are introduced more widely, *Some form of digital inequality will persist and it is possible that those who demand purely face to face interactions will receive a residual service due to the comparatively high costs of the service* (Hardy and Loader, 2009, p664).

Our view is that the benefits of assistive technologies and telecare outweigh the disadvantages and that, given demographic challenges and likely availability of resources, it is inevitable that some degree of use of remote technology will replace some face-to-face interventions, though great care will need to be taken to ensure that this does not reinforce any digital divides. One of the functions of the key messages of this book is to encourage the social work profession to challenge the potential for digital discrimination, and in this sphere part of this process is to ensure that all service users have the appropriate assistance when accessing relevant digital technologies.

RESEARCH SUMMARY

In relation to services for older people, for a deeper understanding of telecare, telehealth, and the potential of these technologies, the review by Blaschke et al. (2009) in the British Journal of Social Work *is a good starting point. In the same journal Hardy and Loader (2009) consider some of the ways that the digitisation of welfare is impacting on older people. Godfrey and Johnson (2009) give a detailed account of digital circles of support and their potential.*

CASE STUDY

The social (net) worker: digital circles of support

The Leeds LinkAge Plus is a collaborative project between the local authority and voluntary and community organisations. One of the main aims is to ensure that older people have access to high-quality and co-ordinated services. To that end a digital information store has been developed to act as a pool of knowledge relevant to local older people and their needs.

The researchers who developed and evaluated the project suggest that the real-life networks or circles of support that surround an older person, including friends, relatives, neighbours, social care workers and community volunteers, can be replicated online in a 'digital circle of support'.

For example, those in the circle of support can use the internet to search for information on the person's behalf. They can seek advice from social networking sites (one example given is of a discussion relating to the difficulties of being a caregiver, hosted on a forum on the website of the organisation Saga). It is also suggested that technologies can be used to improve communication and liaison between those in the circle of support. At a simple level this might involve sending emails to each other. It is suggested that digital social networks be created to improve collaboration and information sharing between members of the network in order to provide the best support to the person concerned.

In this way it is suggested that interactive Web 2.0 technologies can be allied to the more traditional web-based information portals to provide effective mechanisms for getting relevant information from the internet to older people and also for getting those older people to use the technologies more themselves.

In the above example some of the benefits of Web 2.0 technologies are evident. The term Web 2.0 refers to software programs characterised by file sharing and user-generated content, unlike the early websites which were largely textual and read-only. This example also highlights the fact that, while older people may often be fearful of new technologies they do not understand, certain techniques, including the involvement and encouragement of a known person from their peer group, can significantly increase accessibility and use. As a social worker in this field you may be involved in directly or indirectly assisting older people to access such services. If you do work with older people it is certainly worth spending some time researching whether any similar initiatives exist in your locality. More broadly this example can be seen as an example of a community of practice.

Digital technology and social justice

Social work is an activity which is inherently concerned with issues of social justice. A variety of national and international definitions of social work make this clear. While concerns about the use of digital technologies for surveillance and narrow performance management tasks remain valid, it should also be noted that the technologies offer huge potential for enabling individuals and groups to tackle injustice and for providing mechanisms for service users and social workers to find new ways to articulate and represent the needs of the vulnerable. A look at the history of the internet indicates that it has always been a vehicle for collaboration and for development from the bottom up of information and communication systems which are open, democratic and which meet the needs of users.

The affordances of a Web 2.0 environment are leading to new ways of enabling individuals and social movements. Campaigns and challenges to traditional power structures can develop quickly and exponentially with these new methods which allow the rapid dissemination of and reactions to information and new knowledge. Although, as Morozov (2011) has shown in his book *The net delusion*, we should be cautious about imagining that these new technologies will automatically bring about more open and democratic societies, they do have the potential to empower large numbers of people, both in our own society and in less free ones around the world. It might be an urban myth that Twitter was the key player in the Green Revolution in Iran in 2009, and it may be the case that authoritarian regimes can use net technologies to increase repression and surveillance. Nevertheless, there are recent relevant examples of the democratising potential of digital technologies including the role of social networks in bringing information to oppressed populations and in catalysing political change in the Middle East. A healthy dose of scepticism is warranted in relation to technology but this should not obscure to the view of social workers the potential transformative power of technologies when people are enabled to use them widely and effectively. See Table 5.1 for a summary of the potential benefits and problems relating to the use of digital technologies in social work practice.

Table 5.1 Summary of the potential benefits and problems relating to the use of digital technologies in social work practice

Potential benefits

- Allows rapid and convenient sharing of information between agencies.

- Enables people to quickly access large volumes of information relevant to their needs.

- Enables older people and those with disabilities to maintain a greater degree of independence and to more easily find information about things that can help with self-directed support.

- Helps to reduce admissions to hospitals and care homes.

- Allows for the provision of low-cost and confidential online therapy.

Potential problems

- Lack of dedicated access to a computer in an environment that allows for confidentiality.

- Lack of a secure means of transferring information.

- Complex logging on procedures.

- Unreliable systems.

- Computer-based documents and systems that lack flexibility and are too rigid and prescriptive.

- Documents and systems that focus on performance management, rather than on the needs of the service user.

- Time required to input data and commentary into computer-based systems.

- Lack of methods of incorporating users' voices.

ACTIVITY **5.2** REFLECTION ON THE DIGITISATION OF NARRATIVES

A number of authors have suggested that the recording, storage and exchange of large amounts of information using electronic systems has led to a form of practice that favours dichotomous thinking and excludes narratives and accounts of situations that include the ambiguities and contexts of real human lives (Sapey, 1997; Burton and Van Den Broek, 2009; Shaw et al., 2009; Munro, 2011). It is suggested that this may lead to a rigid and inflexible understanding of people. What are the advantages and disadvantages of using standardised assessment forms and computerised systems of information management in social work practice?

COMMENT

A prevailing view is that the advantages of amassing large amounts of information in electronic systems accrue more for managers and those responsible for assuring that targets and performance indicators are met. Social workers often think that the lengthy standardised forms are rigid and inflexible and the time they spend entering data would be better spent on face-to-face interaction with service users or discussion with colleagues and others who are relevant to the case. You may also have noted, however, that electronic data and forms can be very useful in providing the information required for meetings, case reviews, court reports and supervision.

In relation to the above comments research suggests that in the real world practitioners circumvent electronic systems in various ways and use additional parallel systems for recording and sharing information. In the UK and elsewhere practitioners use face-to-face, telephone, hand-written and other electronic communications in addition to the required agency recording systems. You may have hunches and uncertainties about a case; you may wish to discuss tentative ideas with a colleague; you may wish to criticise other agencies; you may know that a family will access everything in the electronic record and there may be sensitive information which, for sound reasons, you do not wish them to see. In the latter case people are also perhaps aware that electronic records have a permanence that other types of communication do not. Although the electronic trail has its advantages it also has pitfalls, as Schonberger (2009) has eloquently illustrated in his book, *Delete: the virtues of forgetting in a digital age*. All of these may provide justifications for recording and communicating outside of the main electronic system within your agency. There may be advantages in operating other communication systems alongside the official agency electronic systems and this is something worth discussing with colleagues and supervisors in your placement or workplace.

CHAPTER SUMMARY

- Rapidly evolving digital technologies are changing social work and other welfare practices in many ways.

- The increased use of digital systems for monitoring, recording and sharing of information has led to expensive systems, a loss of focus on individual narratives and time-consuming processes for practitioners, which do not often lead to better outcomes for service users.

- Digital technologies do have the potential to improve the sharing of information and make life more efficient for practitioners. Particularly with smart use of newer mobile technologies, there is potential to reduce the amount of time spent completing forms, as well as travelling and physically attending meetings.

- Digital technologies are enabling all users of public services to share their stories more easily and effectively.

- Digital technologies are enabling users of services to maintain and increase independence, to facilitate self-directed support and to find information about support and services more easily. Social workers can have a significant enabling role in this process and one of ensuring inclusivity. They can help to ensure that those who are less assertive, less articulate or have less access to digital resources do not miss out, and in this way they can contribute to reducing the digital divide.

- The use of a range of electronic and interactive resources, including 'virtual reality' is likely to spread within educational processes and settings and may feature more in continuing professional development activities.

FURTHER READING

Hill, A and Shaw, I (2011) *Social work and ICT*. London: Sage.

We have referred throughout the chapter to relevant websites and the Social Care Institute for Excellence website at **www.scie.org.uk** is perhaps the most useful starting point for a wide range of further reading, as well as more interactive learning materials.

Chapter 6
Digital literacies for social work education and practice

Introduction

Throughout this book we have been addressing the potential implications of a digital society for social work education and practice and this final chapter examines the digital literacies necessary for functioning in a digital age. You may feel that assumptions have been made about your own levels of digital competence when you started your course. For example, at university there is likely to be an expectation that you will word process your assignments, use presentation software, access digital journals and make effective use of the internet for research. In both placement and practice you will be expected to communicate via email, manage digital records, use a spreadsheet for calculations and know the difference between private and professional practice with regard to the use of social media. We are all feeling the pressure to have mobile phones and be in continual contact via text or to answer emails on the move. Some areas of the country are moving towards a paperless office and are piloting the use of tablet computers for social workers, ensuring that they have access to the internet and digital case study materials while out in the community. Adjusting to digital lifestyles and practices affects us all and this chapter will address some of the prerequisite digital literacies which provide essential support for these new ways of working.

CASE STUDY

iPads in the community

Shuri Curtis takes her iPad to work. She likes the portability; it is much lighter than a laptop and the battery lasts longer. Shuri finds there are lots of advantages to having digital connectivity at all times. She uses the iPad for taking notes during visits and meetings, liking the clear user interface and easy to see on-screen finger-touch keyboard. iPad application programs (Apps) which support file storage and file sharing mean she always has access to the full range of digital documents required in her work and is able to reproduce and edit them if required. A digital stylus tool makes it possible for forms to be signed without the need for printing out multiple documents and carrying them around or having to scan paper copies into digital formats. Shuri says this speeds up some of the administrative aspects of her work, which in turn helps her to feel more efficient. She can meet people at locations of their choice and know that she has instant access to whatever documentation might be required. Shuri finds its particularly useful being able to access key files at home, should she need to. The versatility of the iPad is the best feature. No matter what the task, whether it is giving presentations to colleagues, sharing photographs and video files, or showing and signing documents, the iPad has an App program which supports it. Being able to contact individuals through Skype via the iPad has also proved to be useful.

This chapter will begin with a definition of the term digital literacies and what they might mean for you as an individual student or practitioner. We will revisit the QAA Social Work Subject Benchmark 5.9 which was introduced in Chapter 4. This benchmark covers the ICT criteria in which social work graduates are expected to demonstrate competence and we will be suggesting links to online resources which will support the development of confidence in these areas. We will examine the triangle of competencies which exist between digital practice, reflection and critical thinking, in particular with regard to evaluating the quality of content returned by search engines like Google and resources such as Wikipedia. Digital literacies will be viewed through the lens of 'Threshold Concepts' which have significant links with the development of critical reflective practice. Finally, we will conclude with a review of those specific graduate attributes that are most appropriate for a digital age.

Digital literacies: Definitions

The term 'literacy' traditionally referred to being able to read and write. It is also used in a generic way meaning to be knowledgeable or well educated in a particular subject area. Nowadays, you will often see the word 'literate' attached to areas such as emotional literacy or information literacy. The term digital literacy, or literacies as it is often used in the plural form, can mean a number of different things. These include the ability to locate, organise, evaluate and analyse information using digital technology but there are also broader meanings which take into account the wider influences of location and the social and cultural environment.

> *Digital literacy is fast becoming a prerequisite for creativity, innovation and entrepreneurship and without it citizens can neither participate fully in society nor acquire the skills and knowledge necessary to live in the 21st century.*

> (European Commission, 2003, p3)

Digital literacies are about having individual confidence with technology. This includes the ability to adapt to a fast-changing world where devices go quickly out of date and online content is continually changing the ways in which it is presented. As well as describing the essential capabilities for living, learning and working in a digital society, they are also social practices. This means that we need to see the ways we operate within digital environments as being influenced by the levels of access we have to other social resources. As we have seen in Chapter 3, social exclusion is related to the potential for digital exclusion and access to new digital ways of working cannot be assumed. Government moves towards the delivery of services which are digital by default has implications for citizens unable to participate and these should be of concern for everyone working within welfare and social care professions. The requirement for university graduates to be digitally literate in the twenty-first century is essential but as well as being competent with communication and the management of information, digital literacies must include awareness of digital divides. This knowledge is integral to teaching and learning and professional working practice.

The term digital literacies can be broken down into several different but interrelated component parts. There are 'computer' literacies which include the ability to use digital technology like laptops, social media, mobile phones, mp3 players, ebook platforms and ebook readers. There are 'information' literacies which are about the management of digital information such as how to find, save, share and evaluate digital content. As well as confidence and competence working with digital text, there are also 'media' literacies which involve working with audio and video formats, 'communication' literacies for effective management of social and professional online networks and 'digital scholarship' literacies which are about working effectively within virtual learning environments, understanding copyright and licence restrictions and being able to effectively evaluate digital resources. Finally there are the linkages between digital ways of working and the lifelong learning agenda. We are all subject to the continual processes of learning, and professional development and competency with digital e-portfolio tools can benefit personal planning and critical reflective practice, as well as offering the means of building a digital identity where we can showcase our professional achievements and status.

What is unique about digital literacies is their individual nature. There is no 'one-size-fits-all' definition which fully suits everyone. You can't take a single exam in digital literacies because different people have their own preferences for establishing digital ways of working and different subject disciplines all have individual requirements. No two people will approach digital practices in exactly the same way. You could say your own digital identity is as unique as your handwriting, and in the same way that handwriting cannot be separated from spelling, punctuation and grammar because they are all part of what it means to be literate, so our digital identities are made up of multiple components. As well as being influenced by our own personalities, digital literacies are influenced by broader social practices. This means they are influenced by the environment in the same way that your opportunities to develop handwriting were influenced by your home and your peer group at school. If you think back to when you first learned to write, you may see how the process was influenced by where you lived, the school you attended, your family attitudes, how much you could afford to spend on pens and paper, what your friends said and did, both in school and out, and whatever else was going on in your life at the time. On top of all these external influences were your own thoughts and feelings about the process of becoming literate. You may have enjoyed the challenge of learning to write or you may have preferred diagrams or numbers instead of letters and words. It is the same with digital literacies. We are all influenced by our own environments and by what is going on around us, by what our family and friends are engaging with and the expectations of our places of work and study. We may embrace new digital ways of working or resist them. If we come from a non-digital background, the learning curve will be steeper than for those bought up alongside mobiles phones and laptops. We may enjoy the speed and efficiency of digital ways of working or prefer a slower, more personal approach. We all bring elements of our personality as well as our own past experiences to the computer keyboard and this is where digital literacies become more about our unique individual characteristics than merely a set of skills or abilities. However ambivalent we feel about the wider influence of a digital society, and resent some of the pressures to adopt digital ways of working, we have to become digitally literate graduates, for example learning to recognise the difference between personal and professional online identities and capable of adjusting from one to the other as and where appropriate.

ACTIVITY 6.1 BUILDING A DIGITAL IDENTITY

A photograph album has traditionally told the stories of our lives. Digital cameras have changed this and now we often trust our memories to computer hard drives or carry pictures around on mobile phones. One advantage of the internet is the way in which it has become easier to produce multimedia content. Creating your own digital identity using images and sound can not only be fun but a useful way of improving your confidence with digital materials. Create a five-minute digital narrative or 'story' about an event in your life using text, pictures and sound as an alternative to the photograph album.

COMMENT

Presentation software where slides can be used to build up a storyboard offers a useful basis for a digital identity. Pictures can be sourced from clip art, from royalty-free image sites on the internet, or from your own photographs or video. A narration can be recorded or music from websites which have copyright-free music files. If you use a favourite soundtrack remember that this is likely to be in breach of licence restrictions and should not be made publicly available. Digital narratives are increasingly being used within community and social services as a means of giving service users a voice. For more information on digital storytelling visit www.oralhistory.org.uk.

An increasingly digital society makes demands on both educational and professional practice to ensure individuals and organisations are best equipped to respond positively to these new ways of working. So far in this section we have described digital literacies which apply to living and working in a digital age, in particular where the internet is the primary means of communication and access to information. Social work students have the advantage that specific technology requirements are built into their social work degree and we will look at these more closely in the next section.

QAA Subject Benchmark 5.9, ICT and numerical skills

The QAA Subject Benchmark 5.9, ICT and Numerical Skills (QAA, 2008), lists the digital practices with which all social work graduates need to demonstrate competency. In Chapter 4 we introduced Benchmark 5.9 and discussed how changes over the past decade reflect the constantly changing parameters of society. In this section we will introduce some online resources you may find useful for developing these specific ICT criteria. As you probably know, ICT stands for Information and Communication Technologies. Throughout this book we have preferred the term 'digital technologies' or have referred to 'technologies for information and communication', rather than the acronym ICT. This is because we feel that ICT implies management proficiency with digital data rather than developing a broader understanding of their social impact, which is a key theme of this book. However, in order to stay true to the language of the QAA Subject Benchmarks, we have used the term ICT in the next section of this chapter.

There are six sections to Subject Benchmark 5.9. It is worth noting that while these have been written specifically with social work in mind, they are applicable to many subjects within higher education, especially those containing a practice-based component. The opportunity to develop confidence and competence in each of these areas should be welcomed, not only as essential to your higher education experience, but also as an integral part of your preparation for professional practice. Under each of the headings below you will find suggestions which should be treated as signposts for appropriate resources on the internet where you will find additional information and support.

1. Using ICT effectively for professional communication, data storage and retrieval and information searching

We all need to be able to communicate online in a professional manner but the speed of online exchanges via email can foster carelessness resulting in simple typing mistakes or serious errors of judgement. It is important to use neutral language appropriate to the occasion and take the time to reread emails to ensure accuracy and aptness. The same caution should be applied to online discussion forums or any other digital environment where you are operating within a professional capacity.

Managing personal email is essential if you are not to feel overwhelmed or lose important communications. Email software like MS Outlook contains a range of options for organising your email exchanges. Microsoft offer a number of different Outlook Tutorials which contain video and self-assessment activities on sharing calendars, protecting yourself from junk email, creating email signatures, filing and archiving past messages and ensuring that the emails you send are accessible. Tutorials are available for Outlook 2003, 2007 and 2010. Visit www.office.microsoft.com and search for Outlook tutorials.

Net-etiquette

Guidelines on the use of electronic communication are often referred to as Net-etiquette or Netiquette. When using text to pass on information we are unaware of how the message is being received and unless we take care with constructing content, it is easy to create the potential for misunderstanding. For example, something sent quickly and with intended humour may be read as inappropriate or even offensive by the other person. The recommendations below are designed to ensure effective and non-offensive use of online communication.

- *Treat electronically communicated text in the same way as written text and always check the spelling, grammar and punctuation.*

- *The speed of electronic communication means it is easy to key in text without thinking. Pause to imagine how you would feel if you were the recipient. What might seem appropriate in the moment may not seem so hours or even days later. Give yourself at least five minutes doing something else and then reread before sending.*

- *Where it is appropriate, use emoticons or 'smileys' if you want to express humour, such as : -) or ;-) as they can help ensure the recipient is aware of the intention behind the text.*

- *Avoid using CAPITAL LETTERS as these are considered the equivalent of shouting and the receiver may find your message rude or upsetting.*

- *Keep it simple; make sure your message is succinct and to the point. You are not having a conversation in an email but are conveying a message.*

- *Always be cautious about giving away personal details online because online communication creates a permanent record. Remember all email and other electronic communication will remain stored on university or organisation servers, even after you have deleted it from your account.*

- *Never be offensive or disrespectful about anyone; if you would not say something face to face then do not say it electronically.*

Digital data protection

The ability to manage digital data securely is an essential one, in particular where personal information is concerned. Paper files and records can be locked away in a cabinet and controls imposed over access. Digital data is less easy to control with greater capacity for potential problems. Using ICT effectively means anticipating opportunities for inappropriate access or data being copied, redistributed, lost or stolen while in transit. Following the principles of data protection will help ensure confidentiality and you will become aware of the Data Protection Act (1988) during your social work education. As a social worker you will have access to both personal and sensitive data about other people and have a duty to comply with the data protection law.

Data Protection Act 1998

The Data Protection Act covers both hard copy and digital information. On the Information Commissioners (ICO) website at www.ico.gov.uk the meaning of the word data has been defined and the information below is taken directly from there.

Data means information which:

(a) is being processed by means of equipment operating automatically in response to instructions given for that purpose,

(b) is recorded with the intention that it should be processed by means of such equipment,

(c) is recorded as part of a relevant filing system or with the intention that it should form part of a relevant filing system,

(d) does not fall within paragraph (a), (b) or (c) but forms part of an accessible record as defined by section 68, or

(e) is recorded information held by a public authority and does not fall within any of paragraphs (a) to (d).

Paragraphs (a) and (b) make it clear that information that is held on computer, or is intended to be held on computer, is data. So data also means information recorded on paper if you intend to put it on computer.

The principles of data protection are also listed on the ICO website. When handling sensitive or personal data (see section 3.1.9 of the Data Protection Act for the definition of personal or sensitive data) it is essential to abide by these eight principles. The principles are:

- Personal data shall be processed fairly and lawfully;

- Personal data shall be obtained only for one or more specified and lawful purposes, and shall not be further processed in any manner incompatible with that purpose or purposes;

- Personal data shall be adequate, relevant and not excessive in relation to the purpose or purposes for which they are processed;

- Personal data shall be accurate and, where necessary, kept up to date;

- Personal data processed for any purpose shall not be kept for any longer than is necessary for that purpose or those purposes;

- Personal data shall be processed in accordance with the rights of the individual under the Act;

- Appropriate technical and organisational measures shall be taken against unauthorised or unlawful processing of personal data and against accidental lost or destruction of, or damage to, personal data, and;

- Personal data shall not be transferred to a country or territory outside the European Economic Area, unless that country or territory ensures an adequate level of protection for the rights and freedoms of the individual in relation to the processing of personal data.

The Information Commissioners Office (ICO) website at www.ico.gov.uk contains further information about data protection including links to guidance about controlling personal information and protecting privacy. MIND, the organisation for better mental health, also has a useful online guide to confidentiality and data protection. Visit www.mind.org.uk and search for Data Protection.

Information searching

Using the internet to find information is common practice but the vast amount of content means we need to effectively evaluate what we find in order to ascertain its accuracy and provenance. There are several high-quality online resources which have been designed to offer practical support for developing internet research skills.

The Internet Social Worker is a free online tutorial to help students make discerning use of the internet when researching for coursework and assignments. The tutorial is available from the Virtual Training Suite. Visit www.vtstutorials.co.uk and search for Social Work.

The Internet Detective is a free online tutorial designed to help you develop effective online research skills. Areas covered include those advanced internet skills necessary for university research, the difficulties of establishing online quality controls, how to critically evaluate digital information, and advice on plagiarism, copyright, citation and references. The Internet Detective is available at www.vtstutorials.ac.uk/detective.html.

2. Using ICT in working with people who use services

The relationship between service users and ICT can be difficult. Throughout this book we have stressed the linkages between existing categories of social exclusion and the potential for digital exclusion. Individuals who are dependent on those health and social care services which are evolving into digital-by-default design and delivery may also be those for whom access to the internet is problematic. This is where digital literacies become more than ensuring our own confidence and competence and are about recognising the potential for digital exclusion. As social workers we need to recognise digital inequality and work to ensure individual capacity for digital inclusion is fully realised. One way to be sure we achieve this is to explore some of the digitally inclusive ways of working which can be found online.

AbilityNet at www.abilitynet.org.uk is a national UK charity which supports the use of assistive computer technology for individuals with a diverse range of requirements. They are a useful source of information and advice on the use of access technology and have a YouTube Channel with videos demonstrating the different ways in which assistive communication technologies can be used. Visit YouTube at www.youtube.com and search for AbilityNet.

Barnsley Assistive Technology Centre is located at Barnsley Hospital in the UK. As part of their work with assistive technology they have produced a set of video case studies demonstrating alternative ways of using ICT. Visit www.barnsleyhospital.nhs.uk and select Assistive Technology on their A–Z of services and then select Case Studies.

WebAim is a US organisation which campaigns for an accessible world wide web. Their Introduction to Web Accessibility is an excellent introduction to the potential of the internet for inclusive participation. The video *Keeping Web Accessibility in Mind* offers insight into different user perspectives on the difficulties they face with accessing the internet. It also includes steps we can all take to ensure we do not inadvertently put in place barriers to access when we create digital content. Visit www.webaim.org and search for Introduction to Web Accessibility.

3. Demonstrate sufficient familiarity with statistical techniques to enable effective use of research in practice

Research is about creating new knowledge or increasing understanding of a specialist area. It is an integral part of higher education and, even if you are not collecting primary research data, you may find you become involved in the interpretation or analysis of research findings, for example a literature review or the interpretation of charts and graphs. Data analysis is an important part of managing and understanding digital data and this is where you are most likely to encounter statistical techniques and terminology such as the mean, mode, median and average. Research methods and data collection can be divided into two types. These are quantitative research, with large amounts of numerical data which derives primarily from questionnaires and surveys, and qualitative research which returns textual data from focus groups and interviews. We have already introduced you to the internet Social Worker and the Internet Detective as online resources designed to support the use of the internet for research purposes. The Virtual Training Suite which hosts these resources also contains training materials on using the internet to support the development of social research methods and the understanding of social statistics. Visit www.vtstutorials.co.uk and search for Social Research Methods and for Social Statistics. These tutorials all share common pages at the beginning but then address specific content areas after the introduction.

LearnHigher at www.learnhigher.ac.uk is an online resource centre dedicated to learning development in higher education. Under the area Doing Research there are two interactive resources which support the collection and analysis of research data. Collect This at www.learnhigher.ac.uk/collectthis introduces the basic principles of data collection using a range of methods. Analyse This at www.learnhigher.ac.uk/analysethis is a guide to the analysis of both qualitative and quantitative data.

4. Integrate appropriate use of ICT to enhance skills in problem solving

There are a number of ways in which ICT can support and enhance your abilities to solve problems and Benchmark 5.9 makes specific reference to the following areas:

- Awareness raising, skills and knowledge acquisition.

- Conceptual understanding.

- Practice skills and experience.

- Reflection on performance.

On closer examination it becomes apparent that the criteria are all referring to the proc-esses of critical reflection, for example having accurate details about the issues involved, being able to see the wider picture and all sides of the arguments, to apply theory to practice and critically reflect on outcomes. These abilities are not only key to social work education; the ability to critically analyse and reflect are essential qualities for all areas of professional practice. On your course, you will need to produce evidence of your develop-ment as a learner and a practitioner and this will include relating how you approached different problematic situations. In Chapter 4 we looked at the use of e-portfolios and blogs as examples of the appropriate use of ICT. Free online tools such as Mahara e-port-folio at www.mahara.org and Wordpress blog software at www.wordpress.com offer opportunities for recording experiences using a range of different media and facilities for sharing and for readers to make comments. If you do not have access to these tools, consider using a word processing program to create a critically reflective record of learn-ing and practice. The process of critical reflection on your practice can best be developed through ongoing recording and analysis. To help develop your confidence in these areas, you may find the following online resources useful.

The LearnHigher website at www.learnhigher.ac.uk offers free learning development resources for students in higher education. Select the area on Critical Thinking and Reflection. Materials here are helpful not just for your time at university but also in place-ment and practice. Critical thinking is an example of a transferable skill. This means that resources on critical thinking aimed at academic writing, in particular essays and other assignment tasks, use principles which are also applicable for authenticating websites or developing a critical reflective practice journal.

The Open University provides free online courses, many of which relate to health and social care. The full range can be accessed at www.openlearn.open.ac.uk. With regard to enhancing problem-solving skills, the Open Learn Unit LDT101_2, Extending and develop-ing your thinking skills, may be of interest, in particular Section 8 which looks at Analysis, Argument and Critical Thinking. While the focus is primarily on the analysis of alternative points of view and presenting a balanced argument for assignments, the methods and processes are equally appropriate for the evaluation of digital content and developing the critical reflective practice which is an essential part of the problem-solving process.

5. Apply numerical skills to financial and budgetary responsibilities

As with statistics, you may be wondering why maths and numeracy are appearing in lists of ICT criteria relevant to digital literacies or why they are part of social work at all. The relationship with digital ways of working and numeracy goes back several decades. Small, portable digital calculators have been around for some time and it was inevitable when software was developed to embed computers in the workplace that this would involve working with numbers as much as with text and images. In practice you may find you are required to use spreadsheets in relation to calculating and managing budgets. Spreadsheets have multiple uses and many smaller organisations use them as a database because they support the ordering, searching and extracting of specific data fields. Your digital information and communication competencies will develop on almost a daily basis but you may find fewer opportunities for practising numeracy skills or using spreadsheets. If it has been some time since you last worked with maths, or if you feel you need to brush up your skills, there are free online resources which can be useful for getting up to date numerically.

The Open University provides free online courses, many of which you might find useful for other areas of interest as well as health and social care. The full range can be accessed at www.openlearn.open.ac.uk. Search for the phrase Mathematics and Statistics and browse through the available options.

The LearnHigher website at www.learnhigher.ac.uk offers free learning development resources for students in higher education. Select the area on Numeracy, Maths and Statistics to access resources designed to help you revise or develop numeracy skills.

The Microsoft Office website at www.office.microsoft.com offers free tutorials on all programs within the Office suite including MS Excel spreadsheets. Here you will find a mixture of articles and multimedia tutorials on a range of both beginner and more advanced spreadsheet functions.

6. Have a critical understanding of the social impact of ICT, including an awareness of the impact of the 'digital divide'

This book has been written to support the development of your critical understanding of the social impact of ICT. In an increasingly digital society, there are few ways of working which have not been affected by the affordances of the internet and every year sees new advances with these technologies. In Chapter 1 we introduced the concept of the social shaping of technology. This refers to the ways in which technology is influenced by the environment in which it is produced. We hope that you are beginning to understand how access parameters privilege those with the greatest amount of social capital while excluding those already socially disempowered but who might have the most to gain from being included. The divide between those with easy access to digital technology and those for whom that access is problematic or denied is becoming increasingly significant for social work education and practice as the state moves to digital-by-default public services. If you are still feeling unsure about the concept of the social impact of the internet, it might be worth revisiting some of the earlier chapters in this book, in particular Chapter 1 and Chapter 3.

Triangle of competencies

Applying critical thinking and reflection to the evaluation of content on the internet is a useful opportunity to develop digital literacies. The three elements form a 'triangle of competencies' whereby the theories of critical thinking and reflective practice are applied to digital resources in order to authenticate their content. We will look at each of these in turn.

Critical thinking

In higher education, being critical does not mean criticising someone or something but is about not taking information at face value. You will need to think about a subject in depth and, in particular, try to look for what is not being said. This may seem an odd thing to do but content is often deliberately left out in order to put across an irrational or biased argument and we need to identify instances where this is happening. Critical thinking involves asking lots of questions such as Why? Who? What? Where? and How? It is about examining arguments to see if they are logical, well reasoned and valid. Our conclusions need to follow a similar well-structured approach. In the same way that critical thinking at university does not mean deliberately finding fault, so the academic arguments we create through our critical analysis of content are not about disagreement but about reasons which lead to a carefully considered and well-evidenced conclusion.

Reflection

Reflection involves the ability to look at yourself and your behaviours, thoughts and feelings. It is a personal activity and at first this might not be an easy thing to do. Many students find it takes time to feel comfortable thinking and writing about themselves in this way and for some it can result in the surfacing of difficult emotions. If this should happen, there is always support available for you at university and it is important to know where to find it if necessary. If you are unsure then the Student Union or Student Services will be able to advise you. To help develop reflective practice habits, it can be a good idea to practise writing in a journal or diary which is for your eyes only. If you leave it a few days and then go back to it, you will discover how the intervening time has offered space for reflection and you might see the situation differently. Doing this on your own in private can help to identify those materials which are appropriate for a practice portfolio and those which should be left out. The reflective process works best when it has a critical dimension and as social work students you will be encouraged to become critically reflective not only about your learning, but also about your practice placement and to carry this forward into your professional career. Critical reflection involves the ability to evaluate situations you have experienced and ask yourself questions such as, Why did that happen? Who was involved? Who had responsibility? What would I do differently next time?

Applying critical thinking and reflection to digital resources

During your time at university one of the most frequently used sources of information will be the internet. One established way of finding information there is to use a search engine and Google is likely to be the search engine of choice for the majority of students. The sheer mass of information on the internet means your searches will return many thousands of items. These will need to be analysed in order to identify those which are useful and discard those which are incorrect or have no relevance. The open nature of the internet means there are no systems of quality control; we all have the potential to upload content which can be accurate or inaccurate and many people take advantage of this opportunity to self-publish and promote their own interests. The responsibility always lies with you as the student researcher to tell the difference between accepted academic sources of knowledge and personal opinion. Because we need to learn to use the internet with caution, it is an ideal place to practise critical thinking skills and making effective judgements on the validity of online content.

The first rule of using the internet is not to accept anything at face value but to put into practice your critical thinking skills. There are a number of questions it is always essential to ask. One way of grouping these together into an easy to remember formula is to think of the three headings, Authority, Content and Credibility (ACC).

The authority, content and credibility (ACC) test

Authority The credentials of the author need to be established. Ask yourself the Who? Where? When? and What? questions. Who has written the text? Who owns the site? Is it an individual or an organisation? Where does the author work? Are they representing a known organisation or do they look as though they are a company with a product to sell? What is their field of expertise? Where did their previous employment experience take place? What academic credentials do they have? Where else have they been published? The purpose of these questions is to establish where their authority to write on the subject derives from.

Content Here are some examples of the questions to ask. What evidence can you find for quality control procedures? Is the author backing up their arguments with appropriate citations? Where are the references and can you check them out? Do they refer to personal websites and Wikipedia rather than established, reputable institutions? Do the hyperlinks within the text and the references work or are they broken? What is the purpose of the site? It is giving neutral, impartial information or does it seem one-sided and biased? Is it selling a book or some other product? Is it well written? What is the grammar and punctuation like? The purpose of these questions is to help you to develop the ability to recognise examples of authoritative, academic writing.

Credibility We have already referred to the credibility of the author but there are checks you can also perform on the website itself by asking further questions. When was the information on the page originally written? When was it last updated? What is the website URL or address? Is it a government or academic institution or does it include the name of a free hosting service like Wordpress or Yahoo? Checking the address of a website is a useful process for identifying its origin. For example, .ac.uk or .gov.uk in the URL tells you that the site has academic or government credentials in the UK while .com suggests it is a commercial organisation. Is there a contact email address? Does this use a free email service like gmail or hotmail in its name? You would not expect a professional organisation or institution to be using free software. Asking questions like these will help you to establish the credibility and authenticity of the site.

Practise asking these ACC questions when you visit a website. Not only might you be surprised at how many websites returned by Google fail the ACC test, it is also a useful way to practise and increase your digital literacies. If you always take the time to examine the content of unfamiliar sites and look for the clues which give away its origins, you will become more proficient at distinguishing between reliable and less reliable sources of online information.

RESEARCH SUMMARY

Getting the internet to help you

The mass of information available online can be an advantage and a disadvantage. As a student you will need to learn the appropriate digital literacies for distinguishing valid content from that which is personal and opinion based. Valid content derives from research that has a scientific and objective basis. It contains facts that have been proven and evidence that is measurable through the use of accepted methodologies with a final analysis presented via peer-reviewed publications. Without these checks in place, content may be based on subjective thoughts and opinions and if you rest your own academic arguments on this they will be weakened by their lack of authentic origins. One of the best approaches to developing digital literacies is to take advantage of the resources already available on the internet which have been designed to help you get the most out of researching online.

Google Scholar at www.scholar.google.co.uk will search for scholarly literature such as journal articles, theses, books and abstracts from academic publishers, professional societies, online repositories and universities. You should still carry out your own validation checks but Scholar will significantly reduce the amount of non-academic content returned.

Inside Search at www.google.com/insidesearch is a Google guide for getting the most out of online searching; it includes video tutorials and reference sources for both beginners and more experienced users.

The Internet Detective at www.vtstutorials.ac.uk/detective/about.html is a free online tutorial designed to help you develop effective internet research skills.

BBC Webwise offers a range of resources including articles and tutorials on using the internet. Go to www.bbc.co.uk and search for Webwise.

Wikipedia

We cannot talk about Authority, Content and Credibility of online content without mentioning Wikipedia. This is an online collaborative encyclopedia where anyone with the prerequisite means of access can contribute content or make comments on existing materials. Traditionally, an encyclopedia has been considered to be a credible reference point. For example, during the twentieth century the practice of looking something up in the *Encyclopaedia Britannica* was seen as consulting a reliable source of knowledge and expertise. You may remember the encyclopedia Encarta in the early days of the internet, which was one of the first digital multimedia reference sources published by the Microsoft Corporation and available on CD-ROM. When Wikipedia was first created, the idea of a publicly constructed encyclopedia was dismissed by the majority of academics. They argued that content without the relevant authority could not be considered an appropriate reference source. However, Wikipedia has adapted to early criticisms and survived. Many Google searches now rank Wikipedia high on their lists of returned links. Since Wikipedia first went online, measures have been put in place to impose levels of quality control. Potential contributors are vetted and panels of moderators consider all pages. They highlight content which requires additional clarification and ask for citations wherever comments could be interpreted as personal opinion rather than supported by objective peer-reviewed expertise. However, Wikipedia still needs to be used with caution and this makes it an ideal medium for practising your digital literacies skills, in particular with regard to critical thinking and application of the ACC test.

How to evaluate an article in Wikipedia

All articles, or stubs as they are called in Wikipedia jargon, are moderated by Wikipedia editors who draw attention to perceived shortcomings or problematic areas. When you first go to a Wikipedia page you may see a banner with a warning message such as, *This article is outdated* or *To meet Wikipedia's quality standards, this article or section may require cleanup*. Within the text there may be further comments such as, *This article or section may contain original research or unverified claims*, which highlights the need for further references to reliable source material. These provide clear indications that you should not rely on the content without more research, or consider using an alternative source.

If you find a Wikipedia article with no banners or warning text, does this mean it is safe to use? The answer is still no, not without further consideration. If you really want to use the content, there are a number of steps you can take to verify its authenticity. At the top of the page you will see a number of tabs. The Discussion tab shows the subsequent comments that people have made since the article was written. These may include valid criticisms which raise doubts about the authenticity of certain points. The View History tab will give you a better idea of when the article was written and the dates of any subsequent comments. Both of these will indicate the number of people involved in working on the article and whether or not there appears to be any ongoing disagreement. This can be evidenced not only through discussion comments, but also via the View History page, which will show if there have been repeated deletions and reinsertions that may affect the validity of the content. Large amounts of debate and continual revisions suggest that the topic is a controversial rather than stable one so, again, you should seek an alternative peer-reviewed reference source which has greater academic credibility.

Wikipedia offers its own guide to using Wikipedia for research. This clearly states that responsibility lies with the user to ensure that they do not rely on anything they read in Wikipedia but take steps to ensure authenticity of content.

> *Wikipedia can be a great tool for learning and researching information. However, as with all reference works, not everything in Wikipedia is accurate, comprehensive, or unbiased. Many of the general rules of thumb for conducting research apply to Wikipedia, including:*
>
> - *Always be wary of any one single source (in any medium – web, print, television or radio), or of multiple works that derive from a single source.*
>
> - *Where articles have references to external sources (whether online or not) read the references and check whether they really do support what the article says.*
>
> - *In most academic institutions, major references to Wikipedia, along with most encyclopedias, are unacceptable for a research paper.*
>
> (Wikipedia, 2011)

ACTIVITY *6.2* *A DIGITAL TOOLBOX – WHAT IS IN YOURS?*

Since the advent of Web 2.0 thousands of different digital software programs have been developed. While many of these take the form of games or activities to share with other people, there are others which are specifically designed to help you search for and manage digital content; these include those Applications (Apps) which can be downloaded onto mobile devices. Spend five minutes thinking about the digital tools you have experience with and make a list of those you use most often.

COMMENT

Your list might include the following:

Email (Outlook, Yahoo, gmail, Windows Live)

Browser software (Internet Explorer, Firefox, Chrome, Safari)

Search engines (Google, Yahoo, Bing)

Social networking sites (Facebook, MySpace, Twitter)

Social bookmarking sites (Delicious, Digg, StumbleUpon)

Image sites (Flickr, Picasa, PhotoBucket)

Multimedia sites (YouTube, Windows Media Player, QuickTime)

Retail sites (Amazon, eBay, iTunes)

Wikis, Blogs, ebook readers

Sometimes it can feel easier to avoid new and different ways of working. You might prefer to stay with methods you are familiar with. However, making the effort to try out new digital tools is one of the best ways of developing and enhancing your digital literacies.

Threshold concepts

So far in this chapter, we have shown you how digital literacies are complex, involving lots of different component parts, and we have examined some of these in this chapter. The concept of digital literacies as social practices is one which may be particularly challenging when you first encounter it. This is where the concept of thresholds can be useful. They describe those areas of a topic that are key to understanding. When we are learning a new subject, we need to grasp these pivotal points in order to progress; we must pass over the threshold in order to move on to the next stage. The idea of threshold concepts has been adapted from the study of economics but because they constitute generic stages in learning they can be applied to all subjects. A key theme of this book is the social impact of a digital society, in particular for service users who may be denied access to digital environments, and the implications of this exclusion for social work education and practice. An important part of what it means to be digitally literate is to be aware of the parameters of digital access and not make assumptions about individual use. It is easy to take for granted that everyone can use a computer and access the internet and forget that many

131

people experience multiple layers of barriers such as those we introduced in Chapter 3. Because these ideas around digital disability may be new for many readers, it will be useful to apply the concept of thresholds of learning to the subject of digital exclusion.

A threshold concept has five key characteristics (Cousin, 2008).

1 **Adoption of new understandings** If we have always thought of people using computers and accessing the internet with a mouse for navigation and a monitor which displays content, we are missing a range of alternative access options. Digital data has an inherent flexibility which means is can adapt to multiple delivery modes. For example, digital content can be increased in size, the fonts changed and colours and backgrounds altered to suit individual preferences. All websites should contain keystroke commands which make them navigable with a keyboard rather than a mouse. The technology exists for digital content to be transferred to speech so that users can access websites by listening rather than seeing. There is screen magnification software so that it is possible to zoom in to sections of the screen. A wide range of assistive digital technology caters for users with a range of sensory, physical and cognitive impairments. This potential for customisation to individual requirements means that in theory digital equity is possible. This is an important point to remember.

2 **Irreversibility** Once we understand the power of digital data to be available in multiple formats, and the existence of alternative modes of access and delivery, we begin to see the potential for achieving equitable digital access. Now we can gain a better understanding of the structural dimension to digital exclusion. Rather than using a medical model whereby barriers to digital access are caused by individual impairment, we start to see these barriers as being social in origin. They are external to the individual concerned and are created by a lack of provision for a diversity of need. This paradigm shift is irreversible and once understood it will start to influence our future thoughts. We now have a better understanding of how users of assistive technology are denied access through economic barriers of cost, lack of training and support and exclusive digital environments which are not being designed with the needs of their alternative access in mind.

3 **Revealing interrelatedness** Once we have grasped the fact that the technology exists to ensure digital inclusion, we begin to understand the world differently. We notice how supermarkets and High Street stores only stock standard digital equipment; if we want to buy anything alternative we are limited to specialist retailers. We see how their high costs constitute another barrier to access. We notice how few opportunities there are for training in alternative ways of working in local educational institutions and community centres with public internet access. Support from suppliers is limited and costly. Expensive hardware and software can remain at best underutilised and at worst unused, returned to its box and relegated to the back of the cupboard. You may know instances where this has been the case among your own family, friends and colleagues. We begin to notice features on the internet which we now recognise as being inaccessible, for example videos with no subtitles or captions and audio podcasts with no transcripts. We are making connections which support our new understandings in ways we would have been unable to do before.

4 **Questionable space** Once we understand how inequalities of access prevent people from engaging with digital technology, we begin to look deeper into the nature of the structures which create disadvantage and disempowerment. This may be through applying theoretical models of oppression which we have already encountered or researching into new explanations such as the social shaping of technology. It is important to understand how a threshold concept is never a finished subject; it always contains space within which further knowledge and understandings can be sought.

5 **Troublesome knowledge** Our new understandings may be uncomfortable. For example, if we accept that new information and communication technologies are being socially shaped by the environment and privilege those with social capital, then we may have to ask ourselves what part we might be playing in supporting rather than challenging exclusion. Do we consider providing digital content in alternative formats? What experience do we have of assistive technologies? What is our responsibility for ensuring that where access to welfare services is digital by default, service users are still able to participate on an equitable basis?

You may have noticed how these five characteristics demonstrate connections between threshold concepts and critical reflective practice. At university and in practice placement, the necessary processes of self-examination mean that your learning will not always be easy. Achieving your undergraduate degree is about your own self-development as well as acquiring subject knowledge and expertise. Digital literacies have become an important part of the higher education experience. As a social work graduate you need to be able to show that you can operate effectively within digital environments. As a social work professional, you must be competent with digital practice. You will need to be aware of existing categories of social exclusion and the potential for new instances of digital disempowerment. The social impact of a digital society affects us all. In the final section of this chapter we will look at those graduate attributes that are most appropriate for a digital age.

Graduate attributes for a digital age

The term 'graduate attributes' describes the qualities, skills and understandings that students are expected to develop during their learning. Graduate attributes for a digital age are particularly important. They demonstrate that you have confidence and competence with new technologies and understand their role in the workplace. They should also show your critical awareness of the impact of a digital society, in particular in terms of digital divides. While there are no fixed definitions for graduate attributes with regard to digital literacies, there are categories of competence which cover the most appropriate areas and we will look at these in more detail.

Graduate attributes for a digital age are underpinned with a sound knowledge of a range of information and communication technologies. This will be evidenced by demonstrating core competencies in word processing, spreadsheets, database, presentation and graphical design software with the associated ability to manage digital files and folders effectively. Document sharing and version control are important, as is the capability to deal with a diversity of media formats and to keep up to date with new digital developments. Digital literacies involve learning and research skills, including critical assessment of the validity of online content and the proven ability to effectively search, retrieve, evaluate and cite appropriate digital resources. Graduates are expected to demonstrate evidence of networking and teamwork and in digital terms this can include engaging with online communities of practice and operating efficiently within collaborative mediums such as discussion forums, blogs and wikis. Your self-development and independent learning may be evidenced through personal development e-portfolios. These support the addition of multimedia, which brings further opportunities to develop digital skills and confidence. Effective communication is a necessity alongside the ability to select the most appropriate medium, for example email for professional correspondence, blogging for reflection, wikis for collaborative group work, social media for personal messages and Skype or video conferencing for off-site meetings. It is crucial that you understand the difference between personal and professional identities when you are engaging with digital communication and ensure that you keep them apart. Being conversant with mobile technology is important; in particular the move towards internet-enabled smart phones and tablet computers, which are increasingly being used within practice settings. Finally, a social work graduate should understand how a digital society privileges a narrow range of access criteria leading to the potential for digital exclusion. As the government moves to digital-by-default services this exclusion means that those who are in most need of welfare support are also those who are most likely to have their access to services denied.

You will come across different digital tools for managing your learning and research experiences. Sometimes it can be tempting to resist them, especially if they look as if they are presenting yet another learning curve or offering something you do not feel you need. However, professional practice in a digital society involves working within a range of digital environments. The tools you will encounter during your social work degree will offer useful opportunities for embracing these new ways of working. With continual practice, you will begin absorbing new competencies and picking up transferable skills, often without realising you are gaining valuable expertise. Finally, throughout your time at university, you should be critically reflecting on your digital experiences and reminding yourself of the unequal parameters of digital access which you are likely to be encountering in your social work practice in the future.

CHAPTER SUMMARY

- Digital literacies cover a broad range of competencies which are core to the higher education experience and professional working practice, including the processes of critical reflection whereby we ask the questions and question the answers in order to authenticate our digital experiences.

- Digital literacies are a composite of personal skills and social practices. We are no longer passive consumers of information but active generators of digital content. We need to distinguish between personal and professional ways of operating within online environments and be aware of the parameters of digital access in order to ensure we do not inadvertently compound existing exclusion.

- There is no one-size-fits-all definition of what a digitally literate individual looks like. Instead, digital literacies are unique combinations of our personal preferences and the expectations of those around us.

- Responsibility for becoming a digitally literate student and practitioner lies with ourselves; we need to take opportunities to engage with new digital environments in order to develop the graduate attributes deemed appropriate for a digital age, and to have a critical awareness of the social impact of a digital society and the construction of digital divides.

USEFUL WEBSITES

The LearnHigher website at **www.learnhigher.ac.uk** is an online resource centre dedicated to learning development in higher education. It contains a range of resources, many of which relate to the content of this chapter, including materials on critical thinking, reflection, numeracy, maths and statistics as well as information and digital literacies.

Wikipedia offers its own guidance to best practice when using Wikipedia for academic purposes. This can be found by keying 'Researching with Wikipedia' into the search box on the Wikipedia home page at www.en.wikipedia.org

The lines between traditional information literacies and the newer digital literacies are blurring as more hard copy material is being digitised. If you are interested in finding out more about how professionals manage the mass of information available the Information Literacy website **www.informationliteracy. org.uk** is a practical resource containing news, case studies and examples of best practice with regard to the latest developments in information literacy.

Conclusion

We hope that reading these chapters has led to your developing a greater awareness and understanding of digital issues as they affect society in the early twenty-first century and why they matter so much to the business of social work. While computers, electronic circuits and digital technology might seem to be the antithesis of the care and individual human interaction which is at the heart of social work, we hope you recognise that there are a range of persuasive reasons for social workers to pay attention to digital issues.

At this point we will revisit the content and themes of the book, in order to consolidate your understanding of these issues and the links between them.

In Chapter 1 we discussed how digital information and communication technologies are changing individual lifestyles and working practices. We introduced the concept of the social shaping of technology whereby the internet and world wide web can be seen as mirrors of the society in which they are developed. While there are positive advantages to the ease with which we can communicate and access information in the twenty-first century, there are also negative aspects which we need to be aware of, in particular when working with vulnerable young people and adults. We also need to be comfortable with the difference between personal and professional online identities in a digital society and ensure we keep them separate.

Chapter 2 assessed the way in which public services are moving to digital-by-default design and delivery and how government policy is utilising and being shaped by the prevalence of digital technologies. From the many examples presented it became clear that digital-by-default is not likely to be matched with access by default and those who most rely on public services may also be those who are in danger of being excluded by these digital developments. The safeguards of the law and the role of social work in helping to prevent such exclusion were examined.

The theme of digital exclusion is central to this book and in Chapter 3 we examined the parameters of exclusion in more detail. A social model of digital disability was introduced and parallels were drawn between a social barriers model and the ways in which the design of digital technology largely excludes individuals with sensory, physical and cognitive impairments from accessing a variety of digital resources.

An increasingly digital society is shaping many aspects of modern life including the experience of higher education. In Chapter 4 we examined how engagement with digital technologies has come to play an increasing part in the social work degree programme. The processes of learning, teaching and research have all been influenced by the internet and world wide web. The digital skills adopted during the social work degree will constitute important transferable skills, also known as graduate attributes, which will be necessary for you in your professional practice.

This led us on naturally to Chapter 5 in which the use of digital technologies in social work practice was analysed in more detail. Advantages and disadvantages were examined using a range of examples from typical social work practice settings. The use of technology at all stages of practice was touched on, from student placements through newly qualified status and into established practice.

Revisiting some of the issues touched on in Chapter 4, the last chapter in the book, Chapter 6, examined in more detail the implications of a digital society for university graduates in the twenty-first century. Digital literacies are now as important as literacy with numbers and language. However, added to the confidence and competencies that you need to demonstrate with working in digital environments, it is also necessary to have a critical awareness of digital literacies as social practices and to understand the inequalities created by digital divides. These insights are important in both education and professional practice. They are also essential for a person to become a good social work practitioner and one who can advocate for those who are at risk of being digitally excluded.

In an attempt to condense and encapsulate all of this in some key messages to remember, we suggest that the following three themes are central to the message within this book.

- *Digital-by-default* We are living in an increasingly digital society with digital lifestyles and practices; these include a shift in public and welfare services to digital-by-default design and delivery.

- *Digital exclusion* Digital divides mean digital-by-default services might not reach those already marginalised and disempowered.

- *Implications of digital exclusion for social work* The potential for digital exclusion over and above existing categories of social exclusion will exacerbate already unequal access to resources and become an increasingly common issue within social work education and practice.

We will now summarise the key issues within each of these themes.

Digital-by-default

In an era in which digital-by-default has become a government slogan and the delivery of public and welfare services increasingly takes place online, the issue of digital exclusion becomes ever more stark for those who are reliant on the welfare state. In this book we have included examples of the migration of public services towards digital channels and have illustrated digitally related changes occurring in the way in which citizens interact with government and in the operation of the welfare state. We have also looked at a number of examples from social work practice covering a range of service user groups and settings within which social workers operate. Social workers, who work as agents of the welfare state and who work with those who are socially excluded for a range of reasons, have every reason to become well acquainted with these developments. As a social worker you will need to know how to assist those who are 'digitally excluded'; for example, how to help a person access assistive technologies, or how to support someone in accessing welfare benefits which are applied for and managed using online application systems.

Digital exclusion

Digital technologies, in particular those associated with the internet, have rapidly and radically altered many aspects of life in the late twentieth and early twenty-first centuries and in this book we have attempted to give an overview of their social impact. We have introduced the notion that technology is never neutral but is socially shaped. This means that access to the affordances of the internet and other digital devices often mirrors existing patterns of access to resources. For those with easy access, digital technologies offer many conveniences. However, as with any technology that becomes widely disseminated, there is a danger that those who cannot access it will be left behind. A widening digital divide is creating the danger of the growth of a digital underclass. Throughout the chapters in this book we have returned to the fact that the caseloads of social workers in the future will include individuals who are not only experiencing social exclusion in many ways but are also likely to be on the wrong side of a growing digital divide.

ACTIVITY 7.1 A DIGITAL UNDERCLASS

Ellen Helsper from the London School of Economics has written about the emergence of a digital underclass. You should be able to find this policy brief at www.blogs.lse.ac.uk/ mediapolicyproject. The full title of the piece is: Emergence of a digital underclass. *Read the piece and consider how strong the evidence is for the emergence of a so-called underclass of digitally excluded citizens. What do the statistics say? Considering everything that you have read so far in this text, and the evidence from this paper, do you think this exclusion is likely to increase or decrease?*

COMMENT

You may well be familiar with the concept of an underclass from the media or from social policy lectures and textbooks. Although the concept is contested, it is instructive to consider whether it can be applied to digital issues. We have suggested at a number of points in this book that digital exclusion is likely to remain an issue for millions of citizens. Furthermore, with the move to digital-by-default public services, those who most need access may be least likely to secure it.

The implications of digital exclusion for social work education and practice

One area which has been particularly altered by the introduction of digital technologies is the education sector. As a social work student you will be familiar with the ways in which the content and design of programmes of study at university are increasingly being influenced by the availability of digital resources. We have explored some aspects of these digital ways of learning, teaching and research and introduced you to the idea that uncontrolled access to vast amounts of digital information might be changing the ways in which people think and learn. As a social work student and social work practitioner, you will need to learn to balance the speed of working online with the need for the slower processes of critical thinking and reflection.

The process of education for a social worker is of course a blend of academic learning and practice experience. In this text we have focused on both the academic study environment and the practice-based elements of social work education. Guidance has been given on the ethics of using technologies which may be unfamiliar, and on the need for maintaining a distinction between your personal and professional identities online. We have attempted to offer a balanced view of the potential of digital technologies by discussing examples of how they can improve the lives of service users and social workers, alongside knowledge about how new communication and information technologies can be influential in less helpful ways. Throughout the book we have aimed to elaborate on some of the implications of our major themes, i.e. the move to digital-by-default public services and the implications of digital divides for service users and for social work education and practice. Taken together, all of this requires the development on the part of the twenty-first-century social worker of sound digital literacies. We have explored this notion and elaborated on some of the different digital requirements which are necessary to be an effective and well-informed social worker in a new digital age.

Rapid change is one of the distinguishing features of the modern world, and this is particularly true of developments in digital technology. While the themes and issues which we have covered in this book will remain pertinent for the foreseeable future, technologies can develop quickly and sometimes unexpectedly. As a result, some of the ways in which public services and social work practice will be influenced by new digital developments may evolve in unforeseen manners. A key aspect of being a digitally literate student and social work practitioner is to make sure you stay up to date. We suggest that you regularly consult the following sources, and consider adding the links to them to the Favourites section of your internet web browser.

- The technology area of the BBC news website. Go to www.bbcnews.co.uk/news. Click on the 'Technology' tab at the top of the page for the latest news and views on digital technology developments.

- The BBC weekly programme *Click* looks at the world of digital technology and the internet. *Click* can be watched online for seven days after it is broadcast using the BBC iPlayer facility.

- The website of *The Guardian* newspaper contains useful coverage of digital issues in the technology section. Go to www.guardian.co.uk. Click on the tab entitled 'Tech' and this will take you to the technology news and some interesting technology-related blogs.

- *Community Care*, the magazine for social workers, from time to time covers issues of technology as they directly relate to social work practice. Go to www.communitycare. co.uk. Check the 'Resources' sections as well as the 'Blogs'. Here you can find out how practitioners are grappling with digital issues in their day-to-day practice.

Finally, we hope you have found this book interesting and informative. During the time we have spent writing it, there have continually been new developments in the use of digital technology within education, government, employment and leisure; all of which have been reinforcing the increasing influence of a digital society on day-to-day lifestyles and working practices. There can be no doubt that the affordances of digital communication and information technologies are changing traditional ways of living and working. However, not all of these changes can be described as being beneficial and we have seen increasing concerns being expressed about issues such as online fraud, internet addiction and inappropriate use of social media software such as Facebook. As social work practitioners you will be in a unique position to view both sides of the digital divide. On the one hand, you will need to keep up to date with new digital working practices while, on the other, you will be supporting people who are facing the realities of unequal access to digital resources on a daily basis. We hope this book has helped prepare you for the digital dimensions of your social work degree, your practice placement and finally your career as a social work professional. Whether we like it or not, we are all living in an increasingly digital society and the need to demonstrate a critical awareness of the social impact of the internet, and a range of digital communication and information technologies, has never been more important than it is today.

Appendix 1: Professional Capabilities Framework

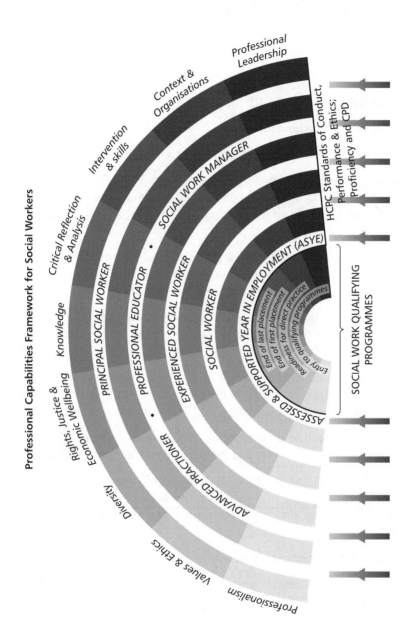

Professional Capabilities Framework diagram reproduced with permission of The College of Social Work.

Appendix 2: Subject benchmark for social work

Subject knowledge, understanding and skills

Subject knowledge and understanding

5.1.1 Social work services, service users and carers, which includes:

- the social processes (associated with, for example, poverty, migration, unemployment, poor health, disablement, lack of education and other sources of disadvantage) that lead to marginalisation, isolation and exclusion, and their impact on the demand for social work services;

- explanations of the links between definitional processes contributing to social differences (for example, social class, gender, ethnic differences, age, sexuality and religious belief) to the problems of inequality and differential need faced by service users;

- the nature of social work services in a diverse society (with particular reference to concepts such as prejudice, interpersonal, institutional and structural discrimination, empowerment and anti-discriminatory practices);

- the nature and validity of different definitions of, and explanations for, the characteristics and circumstances of service users and the services required by them, drawing on knowledge from research, practice experience, and from service users and carers;

- the focus on outcomes, such as promoting the well-being of young people and their families, and promoting dignity, choice and independence for adults receiving services;

- the relationship between agency policies, legal requirements and professional boundaries in shaping the nature of services provided in interdisciplinary contexts and the issues associated with working across professional boundaries and within different disciplinary groups.

5.1.2 The service delivery context, which includes:

- the location of contemporary social work within historical, comparative and global perspectives, including European and international contexts;

- the changing demography and cultures of communities in which social workers will be practising;

- the complex relationships between public, social and political philosophies, policies and priorities and the organisation and practice of social work, including the contested nature of these;

- the issues and trends in modern public and social policy and their relationship to contemporary practice and service delivery in social work;

- the significance of legislative and legal frameworks and service delivery standards (including the nature of legal authority, the application of legislation in practice, statutory accountability and tensions between statute, policy and practice);

- the current range and appropriateness of statutory, voluntary and private agencies providing community-based, day-care, residential and other services and the organisational systems inherent within these;

- the significance of interrelationships with other related services, including housing, health, income maintenance and criminal justice (where not an integral social service);

- the contribution of different approaches to management, leadership and quality in public and independent human services;

- the development of personalised services, individual budgets and direct payments;

- the implications of modern information and communications technology (ICT) for both the provision and receipt of services.

5.1.5 The nature of social work practice, which includes:

- the characteristics of practice in a range of community-based and organisational settings within statutory, voluntary and private sectors, and the factors influencing changes and developments in practice within these contexts;

- the nature and characteristics of skills associated with effective practice, both direct and indirect, with a range of service users and in a variety of settings;

- the processes that facilitate and support service user choice and independence;

- the factors and processes that facilitate effective interdisciplinary, interprofessional and interagency collaboration and partnership;

- the place of theoretical perspectives and evidence from international research in assessment and decision-making processes in social work practice;

- the integration of theoretical perspectives and evidence from international research into the design and implementation of effective social work intervention, with a wide range of service users, carers and others;

- the processes of reflection and evaluation, including familiarity with the range of approaches for evaluating service and welfare outcomes, and their significance for the development of practice and the practitioner.

5.3 All social work honours graduates should show the ability to reflect on and learn from the exercise of their skills. They should understand the significance of the concepts of continuing professional development and lifelong learning, and accept responsibility for their own continuing development.

5.5.2 Gathering information: honours graduates in social work should be able to:

- gather information from a wide range of sources and by a variety of methods, for a range of purposes. These methods should include electronic searches, reviews of relevant literature, policy and procedures, face-to-face interviews, written and telephone contact with individuals and groups;

- take into account differences of viewpoint in gathering information and critically assess the reliability and relevance of the information gathered;

- assimilate and disseminate relevant information in reports and case records.

5.5.3 Analysis and synthesis: honours graduates in social work should be able to analyse and synthesise knowledge gathered for problem-solving purposes, i.e. to:

- assess human situations, taking into account a variety of factors (including the views of participants, theoretical concepts, research evidence, legislation and organisational policies and procedures);

- analyse information gathered, weighing competing evidence and modifying their viewpoint in light of new information, then relate this information to a particular task, situation or problem;

- consider specific factors relevant to social work practice (such as risk, rights, cultural differences and linguistic sensitivities, responsibilities to protect vulnerable individuals and legal obligations);

- assess the merits of contrasting theories, explanations, research, policies and procedures;

- synthesise knowledge and sustain reasoned argument;

- employ a critical understanding of human agency at the macro (societal), mezzo (organisational and community) and micro (inter and intrapersonal) levels;

- critically analyse and take account of the impact of inequality and discrimination in work with people in particular contexts and problem situations.

5.5.4 Intervention and evaluation: honours graduates in social work should be able to use their knowledge of a range of interventions and evaluation processes selectively to:

- build and sustain purposeful relationships with people and organisations in community-based, and interprofessional contexts;

- make decisions, set goals and construct specific plans to achieve these, taking into account relevant factors including ethical guidelines;

- negotiate goals and plans with others, analysing and addressing in a creative manner human, organisational and structural impediments to change;

- implement plans through a variety of systematic processes that include working in partnership;

- undertake practice in a manner that promotes the well-being and protects the safety of all parties;

- engage effectively in conflict resolution;

- support service users to take decisions and access services, with the social worker as navigator, advocate and supporter;

- plan, implement and critically review processes and outcomes;

- bring work to an effective conclusion, taking into account the implications for all involved;

- monitor situations, review processes and evaluate outcomes;

- use and evaluate methods of intervention critically and reflectively.

Communication skills

5.6 Honours graduates in social work should be able to communicate clearly, accurately and precisely (in an appropriate medium) with individuals and groups in a range of formal and informal situations, i.e. to:

- make effective contact with individuals and organisations for a range of objectives, by verbal, paper-based and electronic means.

Skills in working with others

5.7 Honours graduates in social work should be able to work effectively with others, i.e. to:

- involve users of social work services in ways that increase their resources, capacity and power to influence factors affecting their lives;

- consult actively with others, including service users and carers, who hold relevant information or expertise;

- act co-operatively with others, liaising and negotiating across differences such as organisational and professional boundaries and differences of identity or language;

- develop effective helping relationships and partnerships with other individuals, groups and organisations that facilitate change;

- act with others to increase social justice by identifying and responding to prejudice, institutional discrimination and structural inequality;

- act within a framework of multiple accountability (for example, to agencies, the public, service users, carers and others);

- challenge others when necessary, in ways that are most likely to produce positive outcomes.

ICT and numerical skills

5.9 Honours graduates in social work should be able to use ICT methods and techniques to support their learning and their practice. In particular, they should demonstrate the ability to:

- use ICT effectively for professional communication, data storage and retrieval and information searching;

- use ICT in working with people who use services;

- demonstrate sufficient familiarity with statistical techniques to enable effective use of research in practice;

- integrate appropriate use of ICT to enhance skills in problem-solving in the four areas set out in paragraph 6.2;

- apply numerical skills to financial and budgetary responsibilities;

- have a critical understanding of the social impact of ICT, including an awareness of the impact of the 'digital divide'.

Glossary

Assistive technology Any product or service designed to enable personal independence.

Blogs Software for posting text online with a comment feature where readers can reply.

Brokerage Traditionally, brokerage has been used in relation to financial trading and refers to the role of an adviser who facilitates the buying and selling of resources. In relation to social care the term refers to the support given to an individual to help them to identify their own support needs, find out what resources and services are available to them and work out the support package which will best meet their needs and preferences, given the available resources and the support for which they are eligible from the state. There is a lively debate about whether brokerage should form part of the role of a social worker or be best provided independently.

Common Assessment Framework (CAF) The CAF is a shared assessment and planning framework for use across all children's services and all local areas in England. It aims to help the early identification of children's additional needs and promote co-ordinated service provision to meet them. The CAF is a standardised approach to conducting an assessment of a child's additional needs and deciding how those needs should be met. The aim is to support those children and young people who need extra help to enable them to achieve the five outcomes listed in *Every Child Matters* (see below for details).

Cookies Small programs which hold information about the user and are stored as text files on a computer. Cookies save the user having to retype personal information into forms, for example when shopping online.

Cyberbullying Use of the internet for threatening, harassing or embarrassing another person, most frequently through social media, chat rooms and instant or text messaging.

Cybercounselling This refers to the provision of counselling via the internet. Various other terms have been used to refer to similar processes, including e-counselling, internet counselling, cybertherapy, and web counselling. In general the prefix 'cyber' refers to a computer or a network of computers.

Cybercrime Criminal activity using computers and the internet, for example personal identity theft, distributing viruses and illegal downloading of copyright-protected materials.

Cyberethics This terms refers to ethical standards and considerations which apply to information and interactions that take place on computers or computer networks.

Digital-by-default The phrase used by the government to describe the strategy of providing all information and access to services primarily via digital channels.

Digital circle of support A circle of support, sometimes called a circle of friends, is a group of people who meet together on a regular basis to help an individual accomplish tasks or goals. A digital circle of support refers to such a network which 'meets' or interacts online.

Digital divide The term used to describe differential access to computers and the internet. Digital divides are complex phenomena with multiple causes. The phrase refers to both access and quality of access.

Digital underclass This term began to appear in 2011 following research which suggested that a group of people is emerging characterised by long-term unemployment, low skills and lack of access to the internet at a time when such access is increasingly required to engage with the very welfare services that such a group in particular relies upon.

ECDL The European Computer Driving Licence qualification.

EDS (electronic delivery of services) This is almost synonymous with the term e-government, referring usually to the delivery of public, government services electronically, which almost always means via the internet.

E-government The provision of government services via online platforms and interactions. Typical examples include online purchasing of a vehicle licensing disc and online applications for welfare benefits.

Every Child Matters This refers to a policy initiative, begun in 2003, which followed the inquiries into the death of Victoria Climbié and led to the Children's Act 2004. The policy provided a framework aimed at ensuring that all children are able to meet five major outcomes: Be healthy, Stay safe, Enjoy and achieve, Make a positive contribution, Achieve economic well-being. There was a great emphasis on multi-agency partnership working as a means of working towards these goals.

Extra care housing Housing designed with the needs of frailer older people in mind and with varying levels of care and support available on site. People who live in extra care housing have their own self-contained homes, their own front doors and a legal right to occupy the property. Extra care housing is also known as very sheltered housing, assisted living, or simply as 'housing with care'. It comes in many built forms, including blocks of flats, bungalow estates and retirement villages. In addition to the communal facilities often found in sheltered housing, extra care often includes a restaurant or dining room, health and fitness facilities, hobby rooms and even computer rooms. Domestic support and personal care are available, usually provided by on-site staff.

Facebook A social networking website which provides a very popular online platform that allows people to keep in touch easily and communicate with one another online, and to have a presence on the internet without building their own website.

GPS technology GPS stands for Global Positioning System. The system provides information about location and time which is very accurate and is provided by 24 satellites which orbit the earth. There are other similar systems, but the GPS is maintained by the US government. The information provided can be picked up by any compatible receiving device and is now used in many systems, including for the docking of ships, the tracking of car locations, and the location of individuals when wearing electronic tagging devices.

Information Sharing and Assessment (ISA) This policy initiative was closely linked to *Every Child Matters* (ECM) and the Common Assessment Framework (CAF) (see above). The aim was to use the CAF and to have an identified lead professional and a team linked to each individual young person, with very clear policies and procedures for sharing information about the young person.

Information Technology (IT) The accepted usage of this term refers to technologies based on computer systems, used for the production, storage and communication of information. Organisations often use the term to refer to the installation and management of their computer systems infrastructure.

Integrated Children's System (ICS) This government initiative was aimed at developing a system for assessment, planning, implementation and review, which would be common across all agencies working with children and young people. Social services departments were required to produce core information about children in need and their families using common terms. A major feature of the system was that it used detailed computer-based forms and exemplars designed to be shared between agencies using information technology, and this led to the development of major new ICT systems in many authorities.

Personalisation Refers to social policy which is aimed at changing the delivery of public services in a way that gives people using those services more choice, responsibility and control in relation to the services they receive.

Plagiarism Using other people's work and passing it off as your own. The way to avoid plagiarism is to always acknowledge the source of your information and reference these sources correctly.

Portal (or web portal) In relation to computers a portal refers to a website that functions as a single point of access, or gateway, to a large amount of information. Familiar public web portals include Yahoo, AOL, MSN. Many organisations host their own portals which provide a gateway to a range of different types of information in a standardised way. Governments, universities and businesses often have their own portals. In the UK, the Directgov.uk site is an example of a government portal providing a single point of access to a wide range of information and services.

Second Life An online, 3D virtual world launched in 2003. The software allows users to create an avatar which can interact with the avatars of other users. Users can socialise with each other, take part in group activities and create and trade various services, and property, in a simulated environment.

Single Assessment Process (SAP) This refers to an initiative aimed at reducing duplication in the assessment of older people by health and social care professionals. The idea was that information collated by one professional in contact and overview assessments would be used by all professionals involved in the care of the person, while still allowing for further specialist assessments when absolutely necessary, by different specialists.

Social bookmarking Programs which support internet users to share, organise, search, and manage lists of their favourite websites and resources.

Social housing Refers to housing that is let at low rents and on a secure basis to people in housing need. It is generally provided by councils and not-for-profit organisations such as housing associations.

Social media is a term used to describe technologies which are used for interaction and communication between individuals and groups. This is usually taken to mean web-based and mobile technologies and typical examples include blogs and microblogs (such as Twitter), social networking sites such as Facebook, music sharing sites and virtual game worlds.

Telecare This term has been subject to a range of definitions within the realm of health and social care and can refer to a number of uses of technology, in particular those systems which help to signal problems (such as fall sensors); those which help to prevent problems (such as bed sensors which turn on a light to help prevent a person falling when reaching for a switch or getting out of bed in the dark); and those which alert others or provide a warning response in order to reduce harm, including pendant alarms, smoke detectors and heat sensors.

Telehealth Using digital communication and information technologies to provide health care services and access health care education.

Twitter This is an online social network and 'microblogging' service which allows users to send and read short messages, of up to 140 characters. The messages are known as Tweets. Messages sent are public though they can be made private to individuals. Users can sign up to follow particular Tweeters and be notified when they post a message. Launched in 2006, by 2011 the service had 200 million users worldwide.

Universal Credit The coalition government in England introduced the idea of Universal Credit in 2010. The concept refers to the replacement of a number of separate means-tested welfare benefits (including Income Support, Income Related Jobseeker's Allowance, Employment and Support Allowance, and housing benefit) and also the system of tax credits, with a single welfare credit.

Web 2.0 The second stage of web development where the internet changed from hosting read-only static websites to sites supporting file sharing and user-generated content via the text box editor.

Wikis Software programs where users upload information which other users can edit.

References

Adetunji, J (2011) In search of better value. *The Guardian*, 20 July. Available at www.guardian.co.uk

Age UK (2009) *Introducing another world: Older people and digital inclusion*. Available at www.ageuk.org.uk

Alzheimer's Society (2007) *Position statement. Safer walking technology*. Alzheimer's Society. Available at alzheimers.org.uk

Appleton, N and Molyneux, P (2009) *The impact of choice based lettings on the access of vulnerable adults to social housing*. London: Housing LIN.

Auletta, J (2009) *Googled: The end of the world as we know it*. London: Virgin Books.

Banks, D (2011) How stringently should the contempt laws be applied to new media? *The Guardian*, 11 November. Available at www.guardian.co.uk

Barak, A, Hen, L, Boneil-Nissim, M and Shapira, N (2008) A comprehensive review and a meta-analysis of the effectiveness of internet-based psychotherapeutic interventions. *Journal of Technology in Human Services*, 26 (2), 109–60.

Barr, N (2011) The internet will be king for the administration of personal care budgets. *The Guardian*, 17 March. Available at www.guardian.co.uk

Barrett, L (2008) *Healthy at home*. Washington: AARP Foundation.

BBC News (2011) NHS IT debacle shows public accounts committee strength. 25 May. Available at www.bbc.co.uk

Beech, R. and Roberts, D (2008) *SCIE research briefing 28: Assistive technology and older people*. Available at www.scie.org.uk

Bellamy, C (2002) From automation to knowledge management: Modernising British government with ICTS. *International Review of Administrative Sciences*, 68, 213–30.

Berners-Lee, T (1997) *World wide web consortium (W3C) launches web accessibility initiative*. WAI press release, 7 April. Available at www.w3.org/Press/WAI-Launch.html

Berners-Lee, T and Dertouzos, M L (1999) *Weaving the web: The past, present and future of the world wide web*. London: Orion.

Bijker, W, Hughes, T and Pinch, T (eds) (1987) *The social construction of technological systems: New directions in the sociology and history of technology*. Cambridge MA/London: MIT Press.

Blair, T (1999) *Beveridge lecture*. Available at www.bris.ac.uk

Blaschke, C, Freddolino, P and Mullen, E (2009) Ageing and technology: A review of the research literature. *British Journal of Social Work*, 39 (4), 641–56.

Borg, J (2006) *Body language: 7 easy lessons to master the silent language*. London: Prentice Hall Life.

British Library and JISC (2008) *Information behaviour of the researcher of the future*. CIBER Report. Available at www.ucl.ac.uk

Burton, J and Van Den Broek, D (2009) Accountable and countable: Information management systems and the bureaucratisation of social work. *British Journal of Social Work*, 39 (7), 1326–42.

Cabinet Office Central IT Unit (CITU) (1996/97) *Government.direct: A prospectus for the electronic delivery of government services. Cm 3438*. London: HMSO.

Calcraft, R (2007) Blowing the whistle on abuse of adults with learning disabilities. *Journal of Adult Protection*, 9 (2), 15–29.

Carr, N (2008) Is Google making us stupid? *The Atlantic*, July/August. Available at www.theatlantic.com

Carr, N (2010) *The shallows: What the internet is doing to our brains.* New York: Norton and Co.

CEG (2009) *Consumer Expert Group report into the use of the internet by disabled people: Barriers and solutions.* Available at www.webarchive.nationalarchives.gov.uk

Central Office of Information (2007) *Directgov hits one hundred million mark.* London: Central Office of Information.

Commission for Social Care Inspection (2008) *The state of social care in England 2007–2008.* London: Commission for Social Care Inspection.

Cook, J E and Doyle, C (2002) Working alliance in online therapy as compared to face-to-face therapy: Preliminary results. *Cybercounselling and Behaviour*, 5, 95–105.

Cottrell, S (2003) *The study skills handbook.* Basingstoke: Palgrave Macmillan.

Cousin, G (2008) *Researching learning in higher education: An introduction to contemporary methods and approaches.* London: Routledge.

Coyle, D, Doherty, G and Harry, J (2009) An evaluation of a solution focused computer game in adolescent interventions. *Clinical Child Psychology and Psychiatry*, 14 (3), 345–360.

Dardailler, D (1997) *Telematics applications programme TIDE proposal.* Web Accessibility Initiative (WAI). Available at www.w3.org

Davies, A, Hirsch, D and Smith, N (2010) *A minimum income standard for the UK in 2010.* York: Joseph Rowntree Foundation.

Department for Business Innovation and Skills (2010) *National plan for digital participation.* Available at www.culture.gov.uk

Department for Children, Schools and Families (2009) *ICS taking forward improvement plans.* London: Department for Children, Schools and Families.

Department for Culture, Media and Sport (2008) *Delivering digital inclusion: An action plan for consultation.* Rotherham: Communities and Local Government Publications.

Department for Education (2010) *Building a safe and confident future: One year on – Detailed proposals from the Social Work Reform Board.* London: Department for Education.

Department for Education and Skills (2007) *The Common Assessment Framework for children and young people.* London: Department for Education and Skills.

Department for Trade and Industry (2000) *Closing the digital divide: Information and communication technologies in deprived areas. A Report by Policy Action Team 15.* Available at www.socialexclusionunit.gov.uk

Department for Work and Pensions (2010) *Universal Credit: Welfare that works.* Norwich: The Stationery Office.

Department of Health (2000) *National service framework for older people.* London: Department of Health.

Department of Health (2010a) *A vision for adult social care: Capable communities and active citizens.* Norwich: The Stationery Office.

Department of Health (2010b) *Building the national care service*. London: Department of Health. Available at www.dh.gov.uk

Directgov (2009) Directgov site information. Available at www.direct.gov.uk/en/SiteInformation/DG_10036216

Directgov (2011) Directgov site information. Available at www.direct.gov.uk/en/SiteInformation/DG_10036216

Disability Rights Commission (2004) *The web access and inclusion for disabled people. A formal investigation conducted by the Disability Rights Commission*. London: TS.

Ellins, J and McIver, S (2009) *Supporting patients to make informed choices in primary care: What works?* HSMC Policy paper 4. University of Birmingham.

European Commission (2003) *eLearning: Better eLearning for Europe.* Directorate General for Education and Culture. Luxembourg: Office for Official Publications of the European Communities.

European Commission (2007) *Commission staff working document, accompanying the communication 'European i2010 initiative on eInclusion': Impact assessment SEC 1470*. Brussels: European Commission.

Ferguson, I and Woodward, R (2009) *Radical social work in practice: Making a Difference.* Bristol: The Policy Press.

Finkelstein, V (2002) The social model of disability repossessed. *Coalition*, February. Available at www.gmcdp.com.

Fisk, M (2001) The implications of smart home technologies. In Peace, S M and Holland, C (eds) *Inclusive design in an ageing society: Innovative approaches*. Bristol: Policy Press, 101–24.

Gamcare (2010) *We're there when the odds are stacked against you. Annual review 2010.* London: Gamcare.

Gardner, A (2011) *Personalisation in social work.* Exeter: Learning Matters.

Giles, J (2005) Internet encyclopedias go head to head. *Nature*, 438, 900–901.

Godfrey, M and Johnson, O (2009) Digital circles of support: meeting the information needs of older people. *Computers in Human Behaviour*, 25 (3), 633–42.

Greenhalgh, T, Stramer, K, Bratan, T, Byrne, E, Russell, J and Potts, H W (2010) Adoption and non-adoption of a shared electronic summary record in England: A mixed-method case study. *British Medical Journal*, 16 June, 340: c3111.

Gregor, C (2006) *Practical computer skills for social work.* Exeter: Learning Matters.

Griffiths, M (2008) *Social responsibility in internet gambling: Behavioural tracking to help spot internet gamblers.* Manchester: Gambling and Social Responsibility Forum.

Griffiths, M D (2010) Gambling addiction on the internet. In Young, K and Nabuco de Abreu, C (eds) *Internet addiction: A handbook for evaluation and treatment*. New York: Wiley, 91–111.

Hafner, K and Lyon, M (2003) *Where wizards stay up late: The origins of the internet.* New York: Free Press.

Hall, C, Parton, N, Peckover, S and White, S (2010) Child-centric information and communication technology (ICT) and the fragmentation of child welfare practice in England. *Journal of Social Policy*, 39 (03), 393–413.

Halpern, S (2008) Virtual Iraq using simulation to treat a new generation of traumatised veterans. *The New Yorker*, 19 May.

Hardy, M and Loader, B (2009) The informatisation of welfare: Older people and the role of digital services. *British Journal of Social Work*, 39 (4), 657–69.

Hayes, G (2009) *Independent review of NHS and social care IT.* IT Policy Review Group. HC 1015-1. Available at www.e-health-insider.com

Helsper, E, Dutton, W and Gerber, M (2008) *To be a network society: A cross-national perspective on the internet in Britain.* Oxford: Oxford Internet Institute.

Hill, A and Shaw, I (2011) *Social work and ICT.* London: Sage.

Hinduja, S and Patchin, J W (2010) Bullying, cyberbullying, and suicide. *Archives of Suicide Research,* 14 (3), 206–21.

Holdsworth, C (2011) *Regulating digital accessibility and encouraging compliance.* London: Equality and Human Rights Commission.

Holmstrom, C (2011) *Guidance for HE admissions tutors and partners on implementing new arrangements for the selection of students to social work degree courses.* University of Sussex.

House of Commons Committee of Public Accounts (2010) *The national programme for IT in the NHS: An update on the delivery of detailed care records systems forty-fifth report of session 2010–12.* London: The Stationery Office.

House of Lords Merits of Statutory Instruments Committee (2011) *21st report of session 2010–11 drawing special attention to: Draft online infringement of copyright (initial obligations) (sharing of costs) order 2011.* Norwich: The Stationery Office.

Hudson, J (2002) Digitising the structures of government: The UK's information age government agenda. *Policy and Politics,* 30 (4), 515–31.

Hunter, M (2009) A blow for social care: Lack of protection for whistleblowers. *Community Care,* 28 May.

IFSW International Association of Schools of Social Work and International Federation of Social Workers (2001) *Definition of social work jointly agreed 27 June 2001 Copenhagen.* Available at www.ifsw.org/p38000203.html

JISC (2008) *In their own words: Exploring the learner's perspective on e-learning.* Available at www.jisc.ac.uk/media/documents/programmes/elearningpedagogy/iowfinalpdf

Jordan, B (2001) *Social work and the third way: Tough love as social policy.* London: Sage.

Keen, A (2007) *The cult of the amateur: How today's internet is killing our culture and assaulting our economy.* London: Nicholas Brealey Publishing.

Knott, C and Scragg, T (2010) *Reflective practice in social work.* Exeter: Learning Matters.

Lane Fox, M (2010a) *Digital manifesto for a networked nation.* Available at www.raceonline2012.org

Lane Fox, M (2010b) *Directgov 2010 and beyond: Revolution not evolution.* London: Race Online 2012.

La Rue, F (2011) *Report of the Special Rapporteur on the promotion and protection of the right to freedom of opinion and expression.* United Nations General Assembly Human Rights Council 17th Session.

Liebert, T, Archer, J and Munson, J (2006) An exploratory study of client perceptions on internet counselling and the therapeutic alliance. *Journal of Mental Health Counselling,* 28, 69–84.

Livingstone, S, Haddon, L, Görzig, A and Ólafsson, K (2010) *Risks and safety for children on the internet: The UK report.* Full findings from the EU Kids Online survey of UK 9–16 year olds and their parents. Available at www.internetsafety.ie

Lombard, D (2009) Vanessa George case: Plymouth board to hold SCR. *Community Care,* 15 June.

Macdonald, V (2010) Adopted children face anguish as birth parents stalk them on Facebook. *The Observer,* 21 May.

Manovich, L (2001) *The Language of New Media.* London: MIT Press.

Maude, F (2010) *Francis Maude's reply to Martha Lane Fox's letter.* London: Cabinet Office.

Mills, K (2009) *Direct payments for recipients of care and support in Kent.* Kent County Council. Available at www.thinklocalactpersonal.org.uk

Mitchell, A and Cormack, M (1998) *The therapeutic relationship in complementary health care*. London: Churchill Livingstone.

Mitchell, D and Murphy, L (1998) Confronting the challenges of therapy online: A pilot project. *Proceedings of the seventh national and fifth international conference on information technology and community health*. Victoria: British Columbia, Canada.

Moran, M (2003) *The British regulatory state: High modernism and hyper-innovation*. Oxford: Oxford University Press.

Morozov, E (2011) *The net delusion and how not to liberate the world*. London: Allen Lane.

Morris, L and Andrews, P (2011) Social work courtroom skills for a second life. *Technology enhanced learning and teaching recent developments*. The Higher Education Academy. Available at www.heacademy.ac.uk

Munro, E (2011) *The Munro review of child protection final report: A child centred system*. Norwich: The Stationery Office.

Murakami-Wood, D and Ball, K. (eds) (2006) *A report on the surveillance society for the Information Commissioner by the Surveillance Studies Network*. Public Discussion Document. Available at www.ico.gov.uk

Murphy, L, Parnass, P, Mitchell, D, Hallett, R, Cayley, R and Seagram, S (2009) Client satisfaction and outcome comparisons of online and face-to-face counselling methods. *British Journal of Social Work*, 39 (4), 627–40.

Murphy, P. (2008) *Foreword to delivering digital inclusion: An action plan for Consultation*. Rotherham: Communities and Local Government Publications.

National Audit Office (2011) *The National Programme for IT in the NHS: An update on the delivery of detailed care records systems*. HC888. London: The Stationery Office.

National Institute for Clinical Excellence (2006) *Appraisal of computerised cognitive behaviour therapy (CCBT) for depression and anxiety: Decision of panel*. London: National Institute for Clinical Excellence.

NHS Direct (2008) *Disability Equality Scheme 2008–2011*. Available at www.nhsdirect.nhs.uk

Office of the Vice President (1993) *Creating a government that works better and costs less: Report of the National Performance Review*. Washington: US Government Printing Office.

Oliver, M (1981) A new model of the social work role in relation to disability. In Campling, J (ed.) *The handicapped person: A new perspective for social workers?* London: RADAR.

Oliver, M (1990) *The politics of disablement: Critical texts in social work and the welfare state*. London: Palgrave Macmillan.

Oliver, M (1992) Changing the social relations of research production. *Disability and Society*, 17 (2), 101–14.

Oliver, M (2009) *Understanding disability: From theory to practice*. 2nd edition. London: Palgrave MacMillan.

Oliver, M and Sapey, B (1983, 2006) *Social work with disabled people: British Association of Social Workers (BASW) Practical Social Work*. London: Palgrave Macmillan.

Orford, J (2011) *An unsafe bet. The dangerous rise of gambling and the debate we should be having*. Chichester: John Wiley.

Papworth Trust (2010) *Facts and figures: Disability in the UK in 2010*. Available at www.papworth.org.uk

Parrott, L (2006) *Values and ethics in social work practice*. Exeter: Learning Matters.

Parton, N (2008) Changes in the form of knowledge in social work: From the 'social' to the 'informational'? *British Journal of Social Work*, 38 (2), 253–69.

Perry, J, Beyer, S, Francis, J and Holmes, P (2010) *SCIE Report 30: Ethical issues in the use of telecare*. SCIE. Available at www.scie.org.uk.

Pithouse, A, Hall, C, Peckover, S and White, S (2009) A tale of two CAFs: The impact of the Electronic Common Assessment Framework. *British Journal of Social Work*, 39 (4), 599–612.

Porteus, J (2011) *Living well at home inquiry.* All Party Parliamentary Group on Housing and Care for Older People. London: Counsel and Care.

Postman, N (1985) *Amusing ourselves to death: Public discourse in the age of show business.* New York: Penguin.

Public Accounts Committee (2011) *Forty-seventh report reducing costs in the Department for Work and Pensions.* Available at www.publications.parliament.uk

QAA (2008) *Subject benchmark statement: social work.* QAA 236 02/08. Available at www.qaa.ac.uk

Race Online 2012 (2011a) *Getting on: A manifesto for older people in a networked nation.* Available at www.raceonline2012.wordpress.com

Race Online (2011b) *Building the networked nation, the last leap to get the UK online.* Available at www.raceonline2012.org

Rafferty, J and Steyaert, J (2007) Social work in a digital society. In Lymbery, M and Postle, K. (eds) *Social work: A companion to learning.* London: Sage.

Reynolds, D, Stiles, W and Grohol, J (2006) An investigation of session impact and alliance in internet based psychotherapy: Preliminary results. *Counselling and Psychotherapy*, (6), 164–8.

Rodie, S (2009) Whistleblowing by students in practice learning settings: The student perspective. *Ethics and Social Welfare*, 2 (1), 95–99.

Rogers, E M (2006) *Diffusion of innovations.* 5th edition. New York: Simon and Schuster International.

Rogowski, S (2010) *Social work: The rise and fall of a profession.* Bristol: The Policy Press.

Rosenberg, J (2011) *Law in Action. BBC Radio 4,* 7 June. Available at www.bbc.co.uk/news/uk-13666912

RSA (2011) *Online or inline. The future of information and technology in public services.* London: 2020 Public Services Trust.

Sapey, B (1997) Social work tomorrow: Towards a critical understanding of computers in social work. *British Journal of Social Work*, 27 (6), 803–14.

Schonberger,V (2009) *Delete: The virtues of forgetting in a digital age.* Woodstock: Princeton University Press.

SCIE (2011) *Getting connected to e-learning: A short guide for social care providers.* Social Care Institute for Excellence. Available at www.scie.org.uk

Scottish Government (2010) *An assessment of the development of telecare in Scotland 2006–10.* Edinburgh: Scottish Government.

Seddon, J (2008) *Systems thinking in the public sector: The failure of the reform regime and a manifesto for a better way.* Axminster: Triarchy Press.

Selwyn, N (2004) Reconsidering political and popular understandings of the digital divide. *New Media and Society*, 6 (3), 341–62.

Shakespeare, T (2006) *Disability rights and wrongs.* London: Routledge.

Shaw, I, Bell, M, Sinclair, I, Sloper, P, Mitchell, W, Dyson, P, Clayden, J and Rafferty, J (2009) An exemplary scheme? An evaluation of the integrated children's system. *British Journal of Social Work*, 39 (4), 613–26.

Shelter (2009) *Social Housing Factsheet.* London: Shelter.

Skills for Care (2011) *Capable, confident, skilled. A workforce development strategy for people working, supporting and caring in adult social care.* Leeds: Skills for Care.

Social Housing Providers and Digital Inclusion Strategy Group (2010) *Action Plan 2010*. Available at www.raceonline2012.org

StartHere (2009) Available at www.app.starthere.org/sites/web/one/layouts/web/Home.aspx

Stephen, J, Page, J, Myers, J, Brown, A, Watson, D and Magee, I (2011) *System error fixing the flaws in government IT*. London: Institute for Government.

Steyaert, J and Gould, N (2009) Social work and the changing face of the digital divide. *British Journal of Social Work*, 39 (4), 740–53.

Tambini, D (2001) *Universal internet access: A realistic view.* London: IPPR/Citizens Online research publication no. 1.

UK Online Centres (2010) *Digital engagement – understanding customers.* Available at www.ukonlinecentres.com

UPIAS (1976) *Fundamental principles of disability*. London: Union of the Physically Impaired Against Segregation.

Uttley, S (1991) *Technology and the welfare state. The development of health care in Britain and America*. London: Unwin and Hyman.

Van Dijk, J G M (2005) *The deepening divide: Inequality in the information society*. California: Sage Publications.

Van Dijk, J and Hacker, K (2003) The digital divide as a complex and dynamic phenomenon. *The Information Society*, 19 (4), 315–27.

Warren, M (2007) The digital vicious cycle: Links between social disadvantage and digital exclusion in rural areas. *Telecommunications Policy*, 31 (6–7), 374–88.

Warschauer, M, Knobel, M and Stone, M (2004) Technology and equity in schooling: Deconstructing the digital divide. *Educational Policy*, 18 (4), 562–88.

Wastell, D, Peckover, S, White, S, Broadhurst, K, Hall, C and Pithouse, A (2011) Social work in the laboratory: Using microworlds for practice research. *British Journal of Social Work,* 41 (4), 744–60.

White, S, Hall, C and Peckover, S (2009) The descriptive tyranny of the common assessment framework: Technologies of categorisation and professional practice in child welfare. *British Journal of Social Work*, 39 (6), 1197–1217.

Wikipedia (2011) *Researching with Wikipedia*. Available at www.en.wikipedia.org

Williams, M (2006) *Virtually criminal: Crime, deviance and regulation online.* London: Routledge.

Williamson, R (2011) *'Digital by default' should not mean compulsion.* Low Incomes Tax Reform Group. Available at www.litrg.org.uk/News/2011/digital-default

Wilson, D and Jones, T (2008) 'In my own world': A case study of a paedophile's thinking and doing and his use of the internet. *The Howard Journal of Criminal Justice,* 47 (2), 107–20.

Wolfe, M (2008) *Proust and the squid: The story and science of the reading brain*. New York: Icon Books Ltd.

Work and Pensions Select Committee (2011) *The role of incapacity benefit reassessment in helping claimants into employment. Sixth Report of Session 2010–12.*

Yorkshire Post (2011) Head suspended over teacher's Facebook 'insults'. 25 October.

Index

Added to a page number 'g' denotes glossary.